GOVERNING GAMBLING

GOVERNING GAMBLING

JOHN LYMAN MASON *and*
MICHAEL NELSON

A CENTURY FOUNDATION REPORT

2001 • The Century Foundation Press • New York

The Century Foundation sponsors and supervises timely analyses of economic policy, foreign affairs, and domestic political issues. Not-for-profit and nonpartisan, it was founded in 1919 and endowed by Edward A. Filene.

LIBRARY OF CONGRESS CATALOGING-IN-PUBLICATION DATA
Mason, John Lyman.
    Governing gambling / by John Lyman Mason, Michael Nelson.
    p. cm.
    Includes bibliographical references and index.
    ISBN 0-87078-468-4 (pbk. : alk. paper)
    1. Gambling—Law and legislation—United States. 2. Casinos—Law and legis-
lation—United States. 3. Lotteries—Law and legislation—United States. 4.
Gambling—Law and legislation—United States—States. 5. Indians of North
America—Gambling.   I. Nelson, Michael. II. Title.
    KF3992 .M37 2001
    344.73'0542—dc21
                                                        2001002045

Cover Design and illustation by Claude Goodwin
Manufactured in the United States of America.

FOREWORD

The 1999 report of the National Gambling Impact Study Commission, the most comprehensive look at gambling in the United States to date, makes clear one dramatic change that has taken place in America since the mid-1970s: We have gone from a nation in which legal gambling activity was extremely rare—casinos in only one state, a handful of state lotteries, and fairly common, but small-scale, pari-mutuel activities—to a nation in which legal gambling, in one form or another, is permitted in all but three states. Today, tens of millions of citizens engage in some form of legal gambling every day..

Not only has commercial gambling become an immense industry, but state and local governments are heavily involved in the active pursuit of gambling revenues, either directly through lotteries and similar government-operated gambling or through taxes and permit fees for commercial gambling. And, another category of governments—tribal nations—has emerged as a leader in the spread of gambling throughout the nation. Yet, despite the enormous growth of legalized gambling, there has been remarkably little serious research about its effects. The casino industry does support limited research, but, sadly, it has taken a long time to get gambling on the radar screen of the major federal funders of research on addictive behaviors. And the states, despite their expensive advocacy of lotteries, by and large are not doing much.

Those who defend the growth of gambling argue that, in fact, we do know many important things about the impact of legalization. It is, they claim, good for the economy. It legitimizes activity that, in the past, had been underground. They also argue that, for responsible adults, the decision to gamble is a reasonable choice about how to spend recreation dollars. A more philosophical justification often is constructed around the contention that the growth of gambling reflects no more than a democratic impulse expressed in referenda, by state legislatures, and through other political means.

We also know, however, that some gamblers develop patterns of behavior that are destructive both to themselves and their families. And, we know that gambling abuse is highly correlated with other pathologies. Although the more responsible members of the gambling industry acknowledge that there are those who cannot handle the temptations of gambling, the industry's basic position is that problem gamblers are a small minority and can be addressed best by targeted treatment and prevention programs. Some recent research, however, indicates that the number of problem and pathological gamblers in America is growing—a perhaps inevitable result of the increase in opportunities to gamble in recent years. Moreover, the evidence available suggests that efforts to meet the needs of problem gamblers fall far short of what it would take to address the phenomenon seriously.

At The Century Foundation, we have begun an effort to add to the body of knowledge available about gambling's impact on the nation. We cosponsored a conference with the National Center on Addiction and Substance Abuse at Columbia University, "High Stakes: Substance Abuse and Gambling." The conference was aimed at finding ways to understand better the issues involved in creating sound public policy for addressing gambling problems. It drew on the Center's knowledge of the extensive programs that have been developed to deal with other popular activities that have damaging side-effects, such as drinking alcohol and smoking tobacco.

The Century Foundation is, in addition, planning several publications in this area. This volume, by John Lyman Mason and Michael Nelson, professors of political science at Rhodes College in Memphis, Tennessee, looks at two of the major reasons for the rapid proliferation of gambling in the United States: the decentralized nature of gambling regulation and policymaking and the tendency of states to respond to pro-gambling policy changes by their neighbors. Mason and Nelson examine the politics behind gambling at the state, tribal, and federal levels. They also explore the influence of interest groups, the role of campaign contributions, and the ways in which public opinion all help bring about the legalization of gambling—and they reveal how little careful evaluation of costs and benefits lies behind the decisions made.

A second volume, by Rachel Volberg, president of Gemini Research, who has directed a number of studies of gambling and problem gambling since 1986, addresses the darker side of gambling— the prevalence of pathological gambling, its costs to society, and the need for prevention and treatment of the approximately 5.5 million Americans already in serious trouble because of their addiction to gambling.

In the future, we hope to look into some of the other issues surrounding gambling that require more serious attention. As an example, consider the latest growth area for gambling: the Internet. The sheer magnitude of gambling offerings already available on the web provides significant opportunities for people to engage in the kind of behavior that results in problem and pathological gambling. Many Americans do not mind gambling in a controlled environment, where players are protected, the games are fair, and children are excluded. However, gambling at home, whether on a computer monitor or a television screen, raises a number of serious questions such as, Are parents supposed to discourage their children from using a computer in order to shield them from online casinos? More generally, the fact that many Americans want gambling to be legal does not mean that they want it everywhere. Eighteen wheelers are legal, but they do not belong on, indeed often are banned from, residential streets.

Clearly, gambling is a public policy issue in need of serious research and serious debate, and we are grateful to Mason and Nelson for this careful examination of one aspect of the problem— the issue of how we govern gambling.

RICHARD C. LEONE, *President*
The Century Foundation
May 2001

CONTENTS

1

INTRODUCTION

The virtue of book and article titles is also their vice: they are brief and therefore incompletely descriptive. *Governing Gambling* shares, we hope, in that virtue. It certainly suffers from the vice.

"Governing" is deceptive in implying that there is one set of governors. In truth, each of the fifty states has taken a distinctive approach to gambling, ranging from the complete ban on legal gambling in Hawaii, Tennessee, and Utah to New Jersey and Louisiana's embrace of casinos, lotteries, pari-mutuel betting, and charitable bingo. Although state governments are the major actors in gambling policymaking, the federal government also plays a role. Policy toward gambling on American Indian reservations is made collectively by three sovereign entities: federal, state, and tribal governments. Finally, much of the gambling policy that affects the United States is made outside its borders. Hundreds of gambling websites—casinos, sports betting, and lotteries—are now available to American bettors because of decisions by the governments of Australia, Antigua, and other countries to license Internet gambling.

"Gambling" is no less expansive a word than governing. Some forms of gambling are state sponsored, such as lotteries. Others are sanctioned and, in varying degrees, regulated by state governments. These include commercial casinos, horse and greyhound racetracks, and video poker, along with bingo, raffles, pull tabs, "Las Vegas nights," and other games operated by or on behalf of religious, fraternal, and charitable organizations. Still other forms of gambling, including sports betting and Internet wagering, operate largely outside U.S. law.

1

THEMES

Because decentralized governance of gambling is the reality, decentralized politics is our major theme. In this work, we deal with the federal government, the mix of governments that has jurisdiction over tribal gambling, and, above all—because it is the main arena for public policymaking on the subject of gambling—state governments.

But like any theme, the theme of decentralization can be taken too far. The coast-to-coast spread of legalized gambling during the last third of the twentieth century indicates that national trends have been at work. A map of the United States in 1960 would have shown one casino state, Nevada, and no lottery states. To be sure, it would have shown many horse tracks and some dog tracks, but all of the legal betting at that time would have taken place at the tracks themselves.

A map of the United States today would reveal at a glance the extent to which legalized gambling has proliferated. Eleven states, most of them in the nation's heartland, now allow commercial casinos to operate. Twenty-four states have casinos owned by American Indian tribes. Thirty-eight states and the District of Columbia have lotteries, all of them monopolies owned and operated by state governments. Racetracks remain common, but, in contrast to 1960, most of the betting that takes place at these tracks involves either simulcast wagering or, in some states, casino-style electronic games such as slot machines and video poker machines.

In dollar terms, legalized gambling is bigger than movies, bigger than spectator sports, bigger than theme parks, bigger than all the books, magazines, and newspapers published in the United States put together. In 1998, gambling in legal enterprises generated $54 billion in profits to businesses and revenues to government: $17 billion through lotteries, the only form of gambling that a majority of Americans admit to having engaged in, $22 billion through commercial casinos, $8 billion through tribal casinos and bingo halls, $4 billion through racetracks, and $3 billion through other forms of legalized gambling, such as charitable bingo and jai alai.[1]

The trend toward gambling has been national, but, with the exception of tribal casinos, it cannot be traced to actions by the federal government. Presumably, then, a national countertrend could be marshaled in opposition to gambling. As our second theme, we devote special attention to policies that may help to alter the national climate of opinion on gambling by fostering research and analysis concerning gambling's effects on individuals, communities, states, and the nation that will allow debates on the subject to be better informed.

OUTLINE

The chapters that follow consider politics and policy at various levels of the federal system: two chapters examine the states, another looks at tribal gambling, and one explores the federal role. Taken together, these chapters describe and explain the politics of lotteries, commercial casinos and other forms of state-sanctioned gambling, tribal casinos, Internet gambling, and sports betting. Each chapter concludes with a set of policy recommendations to the various levels of government that are involved.

Chapters 2 and 3 address the politics of gambling at the state level. Chapter 2 focuses on state-sponsored lotteries, and Chapter 3 deals with commercial casinos and, to a lesser extent, other state-sanctioned private gambling operations, such as racetracks and charitable bingo. In both chapters, we explain the spread of gambling at the state level partly in terms of what political scientists call "policy diffusion"—that is, the process by which new public policies spread from state to state through imitation and adaptation. Other explanations that are particular to each state's internal characteristics also figure prominently in our analysis. For example, the increasing aggressiveness of lottery advertising is traceable in part to many state governments' dependence on lottery revenues. Similarly, electronic gambling devices and simulcast betting have appeared at racetracks largely in response to the racing industry's claim that without such gambling it cannot remain economically viable. Among the questions we address in both chapters on state politics are what forces explain the spread of gambling among the states and what forces explain the continuing and, in some states, growing resistance to gambling.

Chapter 4 deals with the murky, uniquely multisovereign politics of gambling on American Indian reservations, which began with the Supreme Court's 1987 *California* v. *Cabazon Band of Mission Indians* decision and the 1988 Indian Gaming Regulatory Act and was complicated by the Court's 1996 ruling in *Seminole Tribe* v. *Florida*.[2] For those tribes whose lands are located near population centers and that have been able to negotiate compacts with the states that surround them, significant profits have rolled in from gambling. Other tribes, less fortunately situated or unable because of the *Seminole* ruling to negotiate compacts with their states, have benefited hardly at all. Meanwhile, difficult issues have arisen in the relationship between tribal and state governments over the consequences of gambling.

Chapter 5 concerns the two kinds of gambling—both of them illegal—in which Washington is the most prominent arena for politics and policy. Internet gambling and sports betting have been undergoing close legislative scrutiny in Congress. The federal government is also the locus of much of the policy-relevant research on gambling. All of these federal activities have been influenced heavily in recent years by developments such as the formation of the American Gaming Association, the creation and work of the National Gambling Impact Study Commission, and the increased flow of money from the gambling industry into presidential and congressional campaigns.

Politics aside, the most important federal role in the politics of gambling lies in the area of research. The massive policy changes that have fueled the spread of various forms of gambling in recent decades have far outstripped research-based analysis of the effects of gambling on social, economic, and political life. Active federal sponsorship of such research will enhance our understanding of these consequences in ways that may alter the climate of opinion surrounding politics and policymaking at all levels of the federal system.

2

THE STATES: LOTTERIES

During the thirty-year period from 1964 to 1994, a similar story unfolded in nearly three-fourths of the states: a state constitutional ban on lotteries that had been enacted in the nineteenth century was repealed through a combination of action by the legislature and ratification by the voters. A lottery run as a monopoly by the state government was created, usually with the proceeds earmarked for education or some other specified purpose. If not at the outset, then within a fairly short time lottery sales outlets proliferated into neighborhood convenience stores and other local businesses and the number, variety, and attractiveness of lottery games increased.

Wanting to play, and encouraged to do so by the state lottery agency's extensive advertising campaigns, people of all kinds bought lottery tickets. Poorer, less educated, and minority people bought them in especially great numbers.[1] Although criticisms of the lottery were sometimes heard from both ends of the political spectrum, no serious effort was made to overturn or even restrain lottery operations. Indeed, the state created more—and more appealing—games and undertook more aggressive marketing campaigns. It did so partly in response to the state treasury's dependence on the revenues the lottery brought in, and partly in response to pressures from both the profit-seeking national corporations that helped to develop the games and from the local retail outlets that sold tickets. Only a fraction of the lottery revenues really constituted new spending for the earmarked purpose.

The two processes that drive the politics of gambling—decentralized policymaking and the national climate of opinion—clearly animated the recent spread of lotteries. Each decision to create a lottery was made by a state acting on its own (or in the case of multistate lottery games, by groups of states acting in concert). Yet, as is apparent from the map in Figure 2.1, the rapid spread of lotteries to three-fourths of the states in one-third of a century indicates that a national transformation in public attitudes toward this form of gambling also had occurred. In recent decades, polls consistently have shown strong public support for lotteries.[2]

The elections of 1998 seemed to augur a new spurt of lottery enactments. Although the South has been the slowest region in the country to embrace lotteries—only around half of the southern states have them, compared with 80 percent of the rest of the country—Democratic gubernatorial candidates in Alabama and South Carolina unseated Republican incumbents by championing the creation of lotteries. Politicians in nearby North Carolina and Tennessee watched closely to see what would happen next. Much to everyone's surprise, the lottery was handily defeated by the voters of Alabama in a 1999 referendum, only the second defeat of a lottery at the polls in twelve years.[3] South Carolina approved a lottery referendum in 2000, but Arkansas defeated one. Voters in Tennessee will consider the issue in November 2002.

In this chapter, we chronicle and explain the spread of lotteries in the late twentieth century. We then discuss the issues that dominate the current politics of lotteries. For lottery states, most of those issues have to do with the ways in which their lotteries are conducted. For the thirteen states that do not have lotteries, the main question is whether or not to enact one. As we will argue, the character of the nonlottery states, along with the changing political economy of new lottery adoptions, may be such that the national tide toward lotteries has crested. In the final section of the chapter, we offer recommendations concerning public policy toward lotteries.

LOTTERIES FROM THE COLONIAL ERA UNTIL THE PRESENT

State-run lotteries are a new phenomenon in American life, but legal lotteries of other kinds are not. The modern era constitutes the most recent of three waves of lotteries that have occurred in American history.[4]

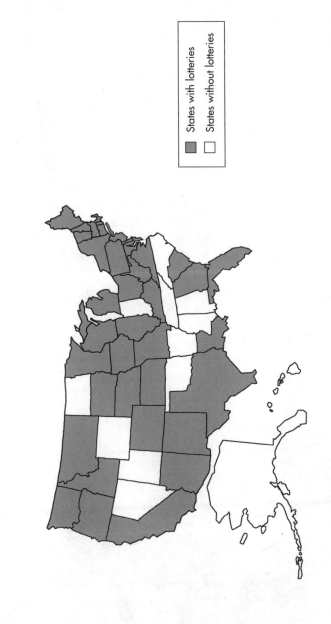

FIGURE 2.1. STATES WITH LOTTERIES

States with lotteries
States without lotteries

Source: Constructed from data in Abbey Begun, *Gambling: Crime or Recreation?* (Detroit: Gale Group, 2000), p. 28.

FIRST WAVE

The first wave of lotteries lasted more than two centuries, from the beginning of the colonial period until the early nineteenth century. All thirteen colonies licensed private brokers to conduct raffle-style lotteries to raise funds for worthy causes, including the construction of buildings at Harvard and Yale, the support of American troops during the Revolutionary War, and, after independence was won, internal improvements such as the Erie Canal. Every Christian denomination except the Quakers conducted lotteries. A textbook used for the training of Protestant ministers at Harvard and Yale during the seventeenth and eighteenth centuries, written by Reverend William Ames, asked, "What is to bee thought of publicke lotteries, wherein many Prizes or rewards are proposed to bee gotten by lot?" His answer: "They might haply bee so ordered that they might be lawful. Namely if there were any need of a contribution to some pious use."[5] Economists Charles Clotfelter and Philip Cook note that, "as with church raffles and bake sales today, the objectives [of these early lotteries] were lofty, the organizers were volunteers, the customers were willing, and the hope was to raise as much money for the purpose as the law allowed."[6]

By the early nineteenth century, however, many lotteries had been transformed into conventional profit-making enterprises. Although regional and national lottery firms with local brokers continued to portray their lotteries as having a civic purpose, they advertised the games with "play-to-win" appeals. Some of these firms turned out to be crooked, even selling tickets for nonexistent lotteries. A "Medical Science Lottery" in New York was revealed in 1818 to be fixed: brokers bought the favor of prominent citizens by telling them the winning numbers in advance. Nineteenth-century reformers lumped lotteries in with slavery, drinking, harsh prison conditions, and other social problems as fit objects for abolition. States, which had never done more than authorize others to conduct lotteries, soon abolished them.

SECOND WAVE

A second wave of state-sanctioned lotteries began in the aftermath of the Civil War. Bereft of other revenue sources, some southern states that had been devastated by the war revived the practice of authorizing private companies to conduct lotteries. The largest of these by far was the Louisiana Lottery Company, which rapidly expanded its operations from Louisiana to the entire country. The national network of railroads and telegraphs that had recently been developed allowed the Louisiana lottery—the "Serpent," to its critics—to market its games through the mail and through branch offices connected to headquarters by wire. Ninety percent of its tickets were sold outside Louisiana.

The other states, distressed by the amount of money that was flowing outside their borders into Louisiana, pressured the federal government to crack down. So did reformers in the burgeoning Progressive movement. In the 1890s, Congress responded by passing its first antigambling statutes. A federal law enacted in 1890 barred from the postal system mail referring to lotteries; an 1895 statute prohibited all lottery activity in interstate commerce. By 1894, no state permitted lotteries to operate legally. (Illegal numbers and other lottery-style games, however, flourished in many places.) All but nine states included lottery prohibitions in their constitutions.

THIRD WAVE

The nationwide ban on lotteries lasted for seventy years. As is shown in Table 2.1 (page 10), the dam cracked in the 1960s, when two northeastern states adopted lotteries—New Hampshire in 1964 and New York in 1967. In the 1970s, the dam broke: twelve states, still mostly in the Northeast, legalized lotteries. During the 1980s, the District of Columbia and seventeen states, representing a majority of every region of the country except the South, followed suit. Six more states, including three in the South, legalized lotteries in the early 1990s. Although only one state, South Carolina, has voted to approve a lottery since 1994, no state has repealed an existing lottery. Together, the thirty-eight lottery states and the District of Columbia include 89 percent of the nation's population.

Certain aspects of contemporary lotteries have remained fairly constant since the third wave of legalization began in 1964. As it happens, all of these aspects stand in contrast to the lotteries of the first two waves. First, the lotteries created in the latter decades of the twentieth century are owned and operated by state governments, not franchised by them to private firms or charitable institutions.

TABLE 2.1. YEARS IN WHICH STATES
BEGAN OPERATING LOTTERIES

STATE	YEAR	STATE	YEAR
New Hampshire	1964	California	1985
New York	1967	West Virginia	1986
New Jersey	1970	Missouri	1986
Connecticut	1972	Kansas	1987
Massachusetts	1972	South Dakota	1987
Pennsylvania	1972	Montana	1987
Michigan	1972	Florida	1988
Maryland	1973	Virginia	1988
Rhode Island	1974	Wisconsin	1988
Maine	1974	Idaho	1989
Illinois	1974	Indiana	1989
Ohio	1974	Kentucky	1989
Delaware	1975	Minnesota	1990
Vermont	1978	Louisiana	1991
Arizona	1981	Texas	1992
D.C.	1982	Georgia	1993
Washington	1982	Nebraska	1994
Colorado	1983	New Mexico	1996
Oregon	1985	South Carolina	2001
Iowa	1985		

Source: Richard M. Pavalko, *Risky Business: America's Fascination with Gambling* (Belmont, Calif.: Wadsworth/Thompson Learning, 1999), p. 42.

Second, voters have been directly involved in the creation of twenty-eight of the thirty-nine lotteries through state referenda. (Passage of a referendum as the final stage in the constitutional amendment process did not become a feature of state government until the Progressive Era.) Finally, the proceeds of contemporary lotteries almost always have been used to meet states' ongoing revenue needs rather than to pay for one-time expenditures. Most of these proceeds have been earmarked by law for a particular purpose. Seventeen of the thirty-nine lotteries specify education as that purpose; other states earmark their lottery revenues for purposes such as transportation projects and senior citizen programs.[7] But economists have found that little if any net increase in spending for an earmarked purpose actually takes place. Instead, most states substitute lottery revenues for money they otherwise would have spent from the general fund.[8]

In other ways, lotteries have been modified during the third wave itself. When the New Hampshire lottery sold its first ticket in 1964, it offered a single, raffle-style game, was modestly marketed, had just two drawings per year, paid out to winners only 35 percent of the total amount bet, and confined ticket sales to racetracks and liquor stores. Within a few years, the New Jersey lottery instituted weekly drawings in which bettors could choose their own numbers; it also raised the payout rate and advertised extensively. New York soon introduced lotto, with its multimillion-dollar prizes, Massachusetts added instant lotteries played on scratch-off cards, and other states inaugurated casino-style games such as keno and video lottery terminals. All of these modifications were made for the purpose of attracting new players and persuading existing players to bet more.

Another modification of lotteries during the third wave concerns the goals for which states conduct them. An important goal for lottery-adopting states in the 1960s and early 1970s, especially in the Northeast and the Midwest, was to drive illegal numbers and policy games out of business by offering similar games legally. In the process, these states believed, they could deprive organized crime of an important source of income. As numbers games continued to flourish, mostly because players could play them on credit and avoid taxes on payouts, states became content to focus on maximizing their own lottery revenues.[9]

A final transformation that has occurred during the course of the current wave of lotteries is from one-state to multistate games. By 1998, for example, twenty-one smaller states belonged to the Multi-State Lottery Association, which runs the famous Powerball game. Seven other states recently formed the Big Game. Powerball and Big Game jackpots now run as high as $350 million. Such prizes are only possible when the betting population is larger than all but a few individual states can muster. By banding together, states are able to entice many people to play who otherwise might not and thus can raise more revenue than they would if they did not act collectively.

EXPLAINING THE THIRD WAVE OF LOTTERIES

By any reckoning, the size and scope of contemporary lottery gambling are greater by far than at any time in American history. Every legal lottery game is conducted by a state agency that was created by elected state officials and, in most cases, approved by the voters in a state referendum. What accounts for the spread of lotteries from one state in 1964 to thirty-eight states and the District of Columbia today?

NATIONAL POLITICAL INFLUENCES

National political influences of three kinds have played a role in the politics of state lotteries. The least significant of these influences has been the small body of federal law that bears on lottery gambling. Constitutionally, it is not clear how far the powers of the federal government would extend if it decided to attack lotteries. The Louisiana lottery was vulnerable to the assault Congress launched against it in the 1890s because it was conducted by a private firm engaged in interstate commerce. It is less certain that Congress's constitutional authority extends to lotteries conducted by sovereign state governments for the purpose of raising revenues for their own treasuries.

Constitutional questions aside, Congress has shown little desire to legislate concerning state lotteries. Its two most recent pieces of lottery legislation were minor and reflect no consistent attitude. The first, which became law in 1988, authorized the states to advertise lottery games more freely than in the past. Although commercial sweepstakes such as those run by Publishers Clearinghouse are governed by Federal Trade Commission "truth-in-advertising" rules, state lotteries are now exempt from such restraints. The second was a 1992 law that prohibited states from offering or allowing sports betting, including sports-based lottery games.[10] In all, the federal government has allowed the states to make lottery policy with little interference.

The activities of national organizations and firms constitute a second, more important national political influence on lottery politics. The National Coalition Against Legalized Gambling (NCALG), an Illinois-based group that was formed in 1994 by Methodist minister Tom Grey, helps to organize opposition to any new form of gambling that a state is considering, including lotteries. National lottery corporations are longer established and have much deeper pockets, however. Although states own and operate their own lotteries, they contract with lottery corporations such as Gtech, Scientific Games, and Automated Wagering to invent games, print tickets, provide software, organize drawings, and make and distribute machines and other lottery paraphernalia. These corporations, regardless of where they are headquartered, operate all over the country. They have had a strong interest in persuading nonlottery states to create lotteries. Recently they have concentrated their efforts on persuading lottery states—especially those with large populations—to expand their menu of games.

The most important national influence on the politics of lotteries has been the climate of opinion. Lotteries entered their period of most rapid expansion in the late 1970s, around the time that antitax sentiment began to peak in modern national politics. In 1978, California voters passed Proposition 13, which placed severe restrictions on the legislature's taxing authority and inspired some other states to enact similar measures. More important, Proposition 13 and its progeny sent a warning to politicians in every state not to create new taxes: only one state has enacted a personal income tax or general sales tax since 1977.[11] In presidential politics, Ronald Reagan was elected in 1980 on the promise to substantially cut federal income tax rates. Reagan not only accomplished this goal, but he also persuaded Congress to cut spending on grant programs to the states. To state governments, caught in a vise between greater revenue needs and widespread opposition to taxes, the lottery seemed an appealing way out: revenue without taxation.

Public support for lotteries in national Gallup polls rose from 61 percent in 1975 to 72 percent in 1982, and has remained above 70 percent ever since.[12] Expert opinion in the 1970s and 1980s concerning lotteries was neither hostile to them nor strongly supportive. For example, although the 1976 report of the Commission on the Review of the National Policy toward Gambling made minor recommendations concerning lottery advertising, its main conclusions were much more in harmony with what the states were already doing. "States should have the primary responsibility for determining what forms of gambling may legally take place within their borders," the commission argued. "The only role of the Federal Government should be to prevent interference by one State with the gambling policies of another."[13]

DECENTRALIZED POLICYMAKING

Within the context of the national climate of opinion and other national political influences, public policy on lotteries has been made on a decentralized basis. Every state that has created a lottery has done so of its own volition. Two main sources of influence on state policymaking have shaped the politics of lotteries within these states: the influence of states' experiences on each other, which political scientists call policy diffusion, and the influence of each state's internal characteristics.

Diffusion. Diffusion theory, as applied to state policy innovation by political scientist Jack Walker, posits that "the likelihood of a state adopting a new program is higher if other states have already adopted the idea."[14] States facing a common problem look to each other for examples of successful solutions, especially to states that are located closely enough to seem comparable. When Wisconsin adopted worker's compensation, for example, Minnesota, Michigan, and other nearby states followed suit.

More than in most policy areas, states have been influenced by each other's experiences with lotteries. In view of the corruption-riddled history of lotteries during the first two waves, states needed to be reassured that lotteries could be run honestly. Not only were the first three lotteries of the third wave—New Hampshire (1964), New York (1967), and New Jersey (1970)—perceived to be honest, but within a few years they also were generating considerable amounts of revenue from their varied menu of games. Just as the lesson spread from state to state that variety was needed to make lotteries lucrative, so did a consensus form that the key to honest lotteries was state ownership and operation.

Once it became clear that lotteries could be run honestly and profitably, the process of diffusion from state to state was enhanced, even accelerated. Because a state loses revenue when its citizens play the lotteries, and thus contribute to the treasuries of neighboring states, it has a strong incentive to try to keep its bettors at home. Examples abound of states legalizing lotteries after one or more of their neighbors have done so. Illinois created a lottery and neighboring Iowa, Indiana, and Wisconsin followed suit; the Florida lottery preceded the lottery in adjacent Georgia; and the Missouri lottery provoked nearby Kansas and Kentucky to enact lotteries of their own. As John Carlin, the former governor of Kansas and a convert to lotteries, said, "not having one when your neighbor has one is like tying one hand behind your back."[15] Political scientists Frances Berry and William Berry have found that the greater the number of lottery states that border on a state, the more likely it is to adopt a lottery.[16]

As states looked to learn about lotteries, there were any number of willing teachers. National lottery corporations were eager to set up shop in a state that was considering a lottery, offering everything from campaign contributions and pro-lottery speakers to technical expertise about how a lottery could be conducted.[17] Perhaps more important, state officials learned from each other. Governors and legislators gather regularly to share ideas about policies, including lotteries, at meetings of organizations like the National Governors' Association and the National Conference of State Legislatures. As Frances Berry has noted, "a national communications network [exists] among state officials in which officials of adopter states interact freely and mix completely with officials of nonadopter states."[18]

Not all the teaching about lotteries has been intentional. Every time a big lottery prize accumulates, regardless of where, newspapers and television stations across the country feature it in their articles and broadcasts. Pictures show the ecstatic winners and reporters breathlessly recount how they plan to spend the prize money. Although these stories are not intended to alter public attitudes toward lotteries, they can have that effect. Readers and viewers in nonlottery states wonder why they can't play lottery games where they live. As voters, they sometimes express that desire at the ballot box.

Internal Characteristics. In addition to the influence that states have on each other through policy diffusion, the second main source of influence on state policymaking is the internal characteristics of each state.[19] Some political scientists have tended to treat diffusion and internal characteristics as rival theories of state policy innovation. In our research, however, we have found that neither offers a complete explanation without the other.[20]

As has been widely established, the economic characteristics of states have affected the likelihood of their adopting a lottery during the third wave. New Hampshire is an extreme case: it is one of only two states in the union with neither a sales tax nor an income tax. Desperately underfunded in the early 1960s, it was the first to turn to the lottery as an alternative source of revenue. But, in varying degrees, every state experienced fiscal problems during the antitax era of the 1970s and 1980s. A pattern emerged: the worse the fiscal health of a state's government, the more likely it was that a lottery would be adopted.[21]

Economic characteristics help to explain why many states have turned to lotteries, but not all states; the politics of each state also matters a great deal. Indeed, the most powerful determinant of whether and when a state has enacted a lottery is the attitude of its political leaders. Initially at least, state political leaders typically disdain lotteries as an erratic revenue source that disproportionately raises money from the poor and lends the moral authority of the state to gambling. In the end, however, and usually in the face of budgetary pressures, they have yielded to a public that wanted to play.

In recent years, what sometimes has tipped the balance toward a lottery has been the election of a governor who campaigned on a lottery plank and made it a priority once in office. In 1987, for example, Wallace Wilkinson, a dark-horse candidate for governor of Kentucky, was elected after running a pro-lottery campaign. Zell Miller was elected governor of Georgia in 1990 on a similar platform. Strangely enough, pro-lottery governors sometimes were more successful when the legislature was controlled by the other political party.[22] Because divided party governments find it difficult to address fiscal problems with controversial spending cuts or tax increases, they may be more likely to enact a lottery as a "painless," even popular tax. In most states, the constitution requires the elected branches to give the last say to the voters in a lottery referendum. Until the mid-1990s, such referenda almost always passed handily.

THE CONTEMPORARY POLITICS OF LOTTERIES

The lottery juggernaut that ran so strongly from 1964 to 1994 has slowed. During the 1970s, states legalized lotteries at a rate of 1.2 states per year. The pace of legalization accelerated during the 1980s to 1.8 states per year. During the first half of the 1990s, six states enacted lotteries, a return to the rate of 1.2 per year. Since 1994, however, only two of the remaining nonlottery states have enacted one.

The contemporary politics of lotteries are different for lottery and nonlottery states. For the twelve states that do not have lotteries, the issue is whether to enact one or not. In most cases, lack of enactment does not bespeak lack of interest. In Tennessee, for example, public opinion polls have always shown strong support for a state lottery and the legislature has voted on at least one lottery proposal in every two-year meeting of the state's general assembly since 1984.

For the thirty-eight states that already have lotteries, the issue is almost never one of revisiting their initial decision to make them legal. Even lottery critics regard the repeal of existing lotteries as a politically untenable goal for the foreseeable future. NCALG, for example, has focused almost all of its efforts on persuading states not to legalize new forms of gambling. Yet because existing lotteries have not been free of problems and controversies, certain aspects of them continue to generate political controversy.

STATES WITHOUT LOTTERIES

Lotteries are strongly supported in public opinion surveys almost everywhere, both in the states that have them and in most of the states that do not. Except for Alaskans and Hawaiians, every American lives in a state that either has a lottery or shares a border with one or more lottery states. Ambitious political leaders in nonlottery states have a strong incentive to urge the enactment of a lottery. Lotteries are a normal activity of state government, they argue, then point to the money that the state loses when its people cross the state line to bet in other lotteries. Arguments such as these keep proposals for new lotteries on the political agenda in most nonlottery states.

In 1998, for example, Democrats Don Siegelman of Alabama and Jim Hodges of South Carolina challenged the incumbent Republican governors of their states by campaigning on lottery platforms. One of Hodges's television ads showed a convenience store clerk wearing a Georgia Bulldogs t-shirt. "Here in Georgia," the clerk said to the camera, "we appreciate you South Carolinians buying our lottery tickets, over $100 million worth. Those Georgia tickets y'all buy pretty much pay for our world-class preschools."[23] Hodges was elected and so was Siegelman, the only two challengers in the country to unseat governors that year.

Yet only South Carolina enacted a lottery in the aftermath of the 1998 elections. Voters in both Alabama and Arkansas rejected lottery proposals at the polls. It is far from certain that they or any of the other nonlottery states—Alaska, Hawaii, Mississippi, Nevada, North Carolina, North Dakota, Oklahoma, Tennessee, Utah, and

Wyoming—ever will enact one. Indeed, the contemporary politics of lotteries in nonlottery states is less favorable to new enactments than at any time since the 1960s. This is true partly because most state treasuries until recently have overflowed with money generated by the economic expansion of the 1990s and the tobacco settlement. But it is true mostly because of more enduring political factors.

One of these factors is that nonlottery states tend to be considerably smaller than lottery states. On average, they each contain 0.9 percent of the nation's population, around one-third of the 2.3 percent average of the lottery states. A small population makes it hard for a state to operate a lottery that will generate substantial revenues for its treasury. Successful lotteries rely on the sort of massive prizes that excite large numbers of bettors to play and play often. Small states, by definition, have a smaller betting population to finance such prizes. Successful lotteries also require that operating expenses remain low. Because of economies of scale, the operating expenses of small-state lotteries tend to run proportionately higher than those of other states.[24] Indeed, even medium-sized nonlottery states, such as Tennessee and North Carolina, now would find it difficult to create highly profitable lotteries. The presence of established lotteries in several neighboring states reduces the likelihood of attracting bettors across state lines and therefore reduces the likelihood of a profitable lottery. For example, one recent study concluded that "Tennessee may have missed the revenue boat by waiting so long to join the lottery game."[25]

A second reason why the current political climate is unfavorable to a renewed spread of lotteries is that not everything the nonlottery states are learning from the lottery states at this stage of the third wave is positive. As is shown in Table 2.2, lottery revenues typically satisfy less than 2 percent of a state's revenue needs—the idea that lotteries can take the place of taxes is illusory. In recent years, research has clearly demonstrated the regressive nature of the lottery as a revenue-raising device. Although roughly equal numbers of people from all demographic groups play the lottery, some play it much more frequently than others. "The heaviest lottery players," Clotfelter and colleagues report, are "blacks, high-school dropouts, and people in the lowest income category." (The data in Table 2.3, page 21, bear out this assessment.) Yet state lotteries depend on the participation of these frequent players: "if *all* players spent the same as the median player, $75 a year . . . , [lottery ticket] sales would fall by 76 percent."[26]

TABLE 2.2. LOTTERY CONTRIBUTIONS
TO STATE TREASURIES, VARIOUS YEARS

STATE/YEAR	PROCEEDS FROM LOTTERY AS A PERCENTAGE OF STATE'S OWN-SOURCE REVENUE[a]	STATE/YEAR	PROCEEDS FROM LOTTERY AS A PERCENTAGE OF STATE'S OWN-SOURCE REVENUE[a]
Arizona		Kansas	
1982	1.0	1988	0.6
1994	0.9	1994	0.8
California		Kentucky	
1986	1.8	1989	0.9
1994	0.8	1994	1.5
Colorado		Louisiana	
1983	1.9	1992	2.1
1994	0.8	1994	1.2
Connecticut		Maine	
1982	2.1	1982	0.3
1994	1.5	1994	1.7
Delaware		Maryland	
1982	1.0	1982	4.9
1994	1.4	1994	2.4
D.C.		Massachusetts	
1984	1.6	1982	1.2
1994	2.2	1994	2.8
Florida		Michigan	
1988	1.5	1982	2.4
1994	2.1	1994	1.7
Georgia		Minnesota	
1994	2.1	1990	0.1
Idaho		1994	0.6
1990	1.6	Missouri	
1994	0.9	1986	1.7
Illinois		1994	1.0
1982	1.0	Montana	
1994	1.5	1988	0.7
Indiana		1994	0.7
1990	1.6	Nebraska	
1994	1.2	1988	—
Iowa		1994	—
1986	0.8	New Hampshire	
1994	0.7	1982	1.0
		1994	1.2

cont. on next page

TABLE 2.2. LOTTERY CONTRIBUTIONS
TO STATE TREASURIES, VARIOUS YEARS, CONT.

STATE/YEAR	PROCEEDS FROM LOTTERY AS A PERCENTAGE OF STATE'S OWN-SOURCE REVENUE[a]	STATE/YEAR	PROCEEDS FROM LOTTERY AS A PERCENTAGE OF STATE'S OWN-SOURCE REVENUE[a]
New Jersey		Texas	
1982	3.0	1994	—
1994	1.9	Vermont	
New York		1982	0.2
1982	1.0	1994	1.1
1994	1.2	Virginia	
Ohio		1989	1.6
1982	2.0	1994	1.9
1994	2.0	Washington	
Oregon		1983	1.4
1986	0.7	1994	0.7
1994	2.5	West Virginia	
Pennsylvania		1986	1.0
1982	2.4	1994	1.1
1994	1.8	Wisconsin	
Rhode Island		1989	1.2
1982	1.2	1994	1.1
South Dakota			
1988	1.1		
1994	3.8		

[a] "State's Own-Source Revenue" excludes external sources of revenue such as federal grants.

Source: Harold W. Stanley and Richard G. Niemi, Vital Statistics on American Politics, 1999–2000 (Washington, D.C.: Congressional Quarterly Press, 2000), pp. 310–13.

Nonlottery states also are able to see, in the experience of their own citizens living in counties that border on lottery states, the extent to which lotteries contribute to gambling disorders and gambling among teenagers.

A third influence on the politics of lotteries in the twelve non-lottery states is the balance of interest group pressures that arise when a lottery reaches the policy agenda. Until recently, national lottery corporations as a matter of course would marshal lobbyists, campaign contributions, and other tools to try to persuade a wavering state to enact a lottery. But, in view of the small size of most of the

TABLE 2.3. LOTTERY PARTICIPATION AND EXPENDITURES
AMONG DEMOGRAPHIC GROUPS

DEMOGRAPHIC GROUPS	PARTICIPATION RATE (%)	ANNUAL PER CAPITA BETTING BY LOTTERY PLAYERS[a] ($)
Race		
Black	48.2	998
White	52.0	210
Hispanic	53.6	289
Other	49.8	295
Education		
Dropout	47.7	700
High School Graduate	52.4	409
Some College	55.6	210
College Graduate	48.0	178
Household Income		
< $10,000	48.5	597
$10,000–$24,999	46.7	569
$25,000–$49,999	57.9	382
$50,000–$99,999	61.2	225
> $100,000	51.0	289

[a] Adjusted for underreporting.

Source: Charles T. Clotfelter et al., "State Lotteries at the Turn of the Century," report to the National Gambling Impact Study Commission, April 23, 1999, available online at http://www.ngisc.gov.

remaining nonlottery states, the financial incentives for these corporations to get involved in enactment efforts have been reduced. In contrast, NCALG is likely to set up shop in almost any state that is considering a lottery in order to rouse lottery opponents from both ends of the political spectrum into action. Liberals may be called to arms by the issues of social justice that are raised by a lottery. Conservatives may be energized by their view that gambling, especially when sponsored by the state, is immoral.

Finally, the national climate of expert opinion has become more averse to lotteries, even if public opinion remains supportive. As noted earlier, the report of the 1976 gambling study commission, which was published at a time when the pace of state lottery enactments was rapidly accelerating, took an essentially hands-off position on lotteries. The 1999 report of the National Gambling Impact Study

Commission (NGISC) was much more critical. The commission rec-
ommended "a pause in the expansion of gambling" in all its forms
and was especially critical of lotteries.[27]

STATES WITH LOTTERIES

The issues of concern for the thirty-eight states with lotteries fit
into three interrelated categories: the goals for lotteries, the advertising of lotteries, and the types of lottery games.

Goals. States with lotteries become accustomed to, even dependent on, the revenues they raise from lottery gambling. Governors
and legislatures impose strong pressures on lottery agencies to raise
revenues for the state treasury at or above the amount raised in the
previous year. They often justify these pressures in terms of the earmarking of revenues: the more people the state lottery agency can
persuade to play (or to play more frequently), the more scholarships
generated or elderly served or other service provided. This challenge
to state lottery agencies is not easily met. From 1995 to 1998, nearly half of the state lotteries had declining revenues.[28]

Clotfelter and Cook have argued for the past decade that states
could decide to abandon what they call the "Revenue Lottery" and
adopt a different goal for their lotteries. The revenue lottery, which is
the model that all states currently follow, is based on the goal of maximizing ticket sales and revenues to the state budget. Clotfelter and
Cook offer instead a "Sumptuary Lottery." States would have as their
goal the accommodation of the public's interest in betting on legal lottery games in a regulated and honest way, but would not encourage
that interest.[29] During the early years of the first two modern lotteries, those in New Hampshire and New York, lottery ticket sales were
confined, in the style of a sumptuary lottery, to locations such as
banks, hotels, and racetracks, which were relatively few in number
and largely unfrequented by children. Since then, however, few if any
states have even considered moving toward a sumptuary lottery.

Advertising. Because their current goal is to maximize revenues,
most state lottery agencies advertise their games with "Madison
Avenue gusto."[30] Indeed, state lotteries are the envy of Madison
Avenue because the federal government places no limit on the tone
and content of state lottery advertisements. By law, the Federal Trade

Commission exempts lotteries from its truth-in-advertising standards because they are activities of state government.

Three lottery states have chosen to limit their advertising and, in doing so, have somewhat restrained their pursuit of the goal of maximizing revenues. In creating their lotteries, Missouri, Virginia, and Wisconsin elected to restrict the tone, content, and frequency of lottery advertising. They instead emphasize information about the rules of lottery games, the probability of winning, and the location of ticket sales outlets.

None of these states has gone so far as to adopt a Clotfelter and Cook–style sumptuary lottery: they all advertise vigorously within the limits they have established for themselves. A recent commercial in Virginia, for example, showed a detective trailing a couple that was shopping for a freezer to replace one that had broken. "Stopping for gas at Lake Raceway, 607 Main Avenue, they spontaneously decided to buy a lotto ticket," he reported. "That night they won half of the $8 million jackpot. This has been a true story brought to you by the Virginia lottery."[31] But the revenues of the Missouri, Virginia, and Wisconsin lotteries, measured on a per capita basis, all fall below the national average.[32] This has made their example unappealing to the other lottery states, whose only goal is revenue maximization.

The North American Association of State and Provincial Lotteries (NASPL), in an attempt to govern its members and placate the NGISC, approved on March 19, 1999, a list of standards relating to the tone and content of lottery advertising.[33] However, NASPL has no enforcement power over state lottery agencies.

Games. The goal of state lotteries to maximize revenues not only influences the tone and content of advertisements but also the types of games offered. The two most recent innovations in state lotteries are video lottery terminals (VLTs) and multistate lottery games. States with lotteries face a decision about whether and how much to participate in these new activities.

VLTs are electronic gaming devices that have appealing graphics, allow players to know instantly if they have won, and, because of these features, appear to be one of the most addictive forms of gambling. In the states where they are legal (and in some states where they are not), VLTs can be found in many venues that children frequent, especially convenience stores.

Regardless of these concerns, VLTs are highly profitable. As noted earlier, in most recent years lottery revenues have fallen in nearly one-half of the states. However, the five states with VLTs have experienced average annual growth rates of 9 to 26 percent.[34] Besides profitability, VLT states share another common feature: they are all states with small populations (Delaware, Oregon, Rhode Island, South Dakota, and West Virginia). VLTs are an option particularly tempting to small states because in their efforts to increase lottery sales, these states must compensate for their smaller grand prizes and pools of bettors.

Another innovation in lottery games also was begun by smaller states: multistate games. Maine, New Hampshire, and Vermont offered the first multistate lottery. The District of Columbia joined forces with five states in 1988 to run the LottoAmerica game, which had a population base of twelve million.[35] The most recent of these games are the Powerball lottery, which encompasses a combined population of fifty-eight million in twenty-one mostly smaller states, and the Big Game, a consortium of seven large states with a population of fifty-six million.

When jackpots reach nine figures, and certainly when they pass the $300 million mark, as a $363 million Big Game drawing did in May 2000, these multistate games lure many people to gamble who otherwise would not. As a result, the state lotteries that participate in multistate games are more profitable than they would be if they did not join forces with other states. No legal barrier prevents the largest lottery states, such as California and New York, from creating their own multistate lottery. For that matter, there is no legal barrier to all lottery states joining together for what would amount to a national lottery.

POLICY RECOMMENDATIONS

Lotteries are the most popular form of gambling and the most popular method governments use to raise revenue. During the 1970s and 1980s, they helped to provide, at least in a small way, a politically feasible means for states to continue satisfying public demands for government services at a time when federal grant money was declining and the voters were strongly opposed to new state taxes. Lotteries also were the vehicle that some states employed to do important and worthwhile things. The HOPE scholarship program in Georgia, for example, which pays the tuition of any A or B student in the state who attends a public university, is financed by lottery-generated dollars. Pennsylvania seems to have much better funded programs for senior citizens than it would have without its lottery.[36]

On balance, however, lotteries are bad public policy. They are a means of raising revenue for state governments whose regressivity makes the sales tax look progressive. The 20 percent of lottery players who account for 82 percent of lottery ticket sales are disproportionately black, poor, and uneducated.[37] With few exceptions, lotteries use their freedom from federal regulation to advertise their games misleadingly, creating the impression that the odds of winning are good and that playing the lottery is a sensible way to enhance one's financial status. The presence of lottery tickets alongside candy and crackers in neighborhood convenience stores places lotteries directly in contact with children, who often are able to evade the law and buy lottery tickets. In lottery states, around one-third of high school students report having bought tickets. In Massachusetts, the attorney general found that children as young as nine were able to buy lottery tickets in 80 percent of their attempts. By the time they were high school seniors, 75 percent reported having played the lottery.[38]

Still worse, as government-owned and -operated enterprises, lotteries put the state into the business of persuading people to gamble. In doing so they encourage not hard work and saving as strategies for success, but luck. "When I was younger I suppose I could have done more to plan my future," says a smiling young man in a commercial for the Connecticut lottery. "But I didn't. I guess I could have put some money aside. But I didn't. Or I could have made some smart investments. But I didn't. Heck, I could have bought a one-dollar Connecticut lotto ticket, won a jackpot worth millions, and gotten a nice big check every year for twenty years. And I did! I won!" As if that were not misleading enough, the commercial ended with a voice-over saying, "Overall chance of winning is one in thirty." In truth, that was the chance of winning a small prize in an instant lottery, not "a jackpot worth millions."[39]

Perhaps worst of all, the business that the lottery puts states into is one that generates its own dynamic of increasing regressivity and deceptiveness. States come to depend on revenues from lottery games as part of their ongoing budgets. A downward cycle ensues. People get bored playing the same games over and over again. Ticket sales and revenues to the state treasury go down. State lottery agencies are pressured to ramp up their advertising, much of it designed to persuade those who already play a great deal to play a great deal more. The agencies adopt new games that are even more enticing: the monthly drawing has given way to the daily drawing, the instant scratch-off game, and lotto. The five states that have gone so far as to market slot-machine-style VLTs have experienced sharp increases in revenues to their treasuries. As new games cause revenues to go up, states come to depend even more on lottery dollars to continue providing services, and the cycle begins again.

At the moment, and for the foreseeable future, lotteries seem politically impregnable in the states that have them. No state that has created a lottery during the third wave of lottery enactments has seriously considered repealing it. But the very fact that two previous waves have crested and receded is evidence that lotteries need not last forever. Both the first and second waves foundered on the shoals of their own corrupt practices and on broad movements of social reform. Although states in the third wave have addressed the corruption issue by directly owning and operating lotteries, no system is immune from abuse.[40] Similarly, politics as usual in America periodically gives way to national eras of civic reform.[41] Somewhere beyond the political horizon the national climate of opinion may change in ways that cause lotteries to be abolished wherever they exist.

We welcome the arrival of that day. In the meantime, acknowledging the decentralized nature of lottery policymaking, we offer recommendations that are of more immediate applicability.[42] To states that do not have lotteries, we recommend that they refuse to enact them in any form. To states that have lotteries, we recommend reforms in the areas of goals, advertising, and games.

GOALS

We recommend that lottery states substantially reconceive the basic goal of their lotteries. Instead of regarding lotteries entirely as means of raising revenue, states should run them in much the same way that many states now operate liquor stores—that is, through a limited number of establishments, owned and operated as monopolies by the state, whose purpose is to offer people a service without encouraging them to use it. This recommendation is not only consistent with Clotfelter and Cook's understanding of a sumptuary lottery, it also accords with one of the founding rationales of the third wave of lotteries, which was to have the state regulate and profit modestly from an activity in which people already were engaging through illegal numbers-style games.

To be sure, even lotteries with this more restrained goal will leave states in the business of offering their people a service that will harm some of them. Those who are prone to gambling disorders will continue to lose much of their money to their own governments. Therefore, we recommend that states earmark a share of the revenues they earn from their lotteries for research about and treatment of gambling disorders.

Earmarking, for education and other purposes, is already a goal of most states with lotteries. In all but ten states, lotteries were created with the promise that their revenues would be devoted to funding a particular activity of government. Most states have betrayed that promise by substituting revenues from the lottery for revenues that otherwise would have been spent from the general fund. Apart from the question of whether earmarking is a good practice or not, when elected governments fail to abide by their own laws, they violate democratic norms.

ADVERTISING

Advertising by state lottery agencies needs to be much more responsible than it is now.[43] As a beginning, we recommend that states mandate that their lottery agencies adopt in full the advertising standards that NASPL published in 1999 for its members. These standards concern the tone and content of advertising, advertising to minors, information about lottery games, and the beneficiaries of lottery proceeds. They specify, for example, that lottery advertisements "should not encourage people to play excessively or beyond their means"; nor should advertisements present games as "a potential means of relieving any person's financial or personal difficulties."

The NASPL standards constitute a good beginning, but do not go far enough. The standard concerning "game information" is especially inadequate: "Odds of winning must be readily available to the public and be clearly stated." We recommend that clear and accurate information about the probability of winning each game and the share of each dollar wagered that the state pays out in prizes not only be available to those who request it but also be displayed prominently in all lottery advertising.

In addition, the only NASPL standard governing advertising targeted at particular groups concerns minors. We recommend that any form of advertising that is targeted at any vulnerable group be forbidden, especially ads aimed at those whom research has shown to be the most prone to excessive gambling on lotteries: the poor, minorities, and the less educated.

GAMES

Still with an eye on those prone to excessive gambling, we recommend that lottery states without VLTs stay that way and that states that allow VLTs make them illegal. The speed of play, appealing graphics, and ubiquity of these machines in the states where they are legal make them unnecessarily tempting to both minors and those who suffer from gambling disorders, two groups that states must not take advantage of in their pursuit of revenues. Moreover, because these machines are made with the intention of looking and sounding like slot machines, states that have legalized VLTs but have not legalized casinos are entering a gray area between what their policies allow and what their lottery agencies practice.

We argued earlier that states would better serve their citizens by forgoing the revenue-maximizing lottery in favor of one that satisfied gambling desires without fostering them. Because multistate lottery games such as Powerball exist only to encourage more play and thus gain more revenue, we recommend that states abandon multistate lottery games. By dangling the carrot of a $350 million cash prize, which only multistate lotteries have the pool of bettors to finance, state governments—the would-be protectors of the public interest—send the wrong signal with perfect clarity: gamble your way to success rather than work for it.

3

THE STATES:
COMMERCIAL CASINOS AND
OTHER FORMS OF GAMBLING

The varieties of gambling that states allow fall into two categories. The first is *state-sponsored gambling*—that is, gambling operations that are owned and operated by state governments. At present, this category includes only lotteries, which are dealt with in Chapter 2. The other category includes several forms of *state-sanctioned gambling*. Commercial casinos; pari-mutuel betting on horse racing, dog racing, and jai alai; card rooms; electronic gaming devices; and charitable bingo and other charitable games are forms of gambling that states regulate rather than own and operate. These forms of gambling are dealt with in this chapter, with an emphasis on commercial casinos.

For many years, casinos were the least important form of state-sanctioned gambling. In 1931 Nevada legalized commercial casinos. But in that same Depression-era decade, more than twenty state governments legalized and taxed pari-mutuel betting on horse racing in a quest for new revenues. All but a handful of other states followed suit in the 1940s and 1950s. By 2000, horse race gambling was legal at more than 150 tracks in forty-two states. As recently as the 1970s, horse racing was the most popular legal form of gambling in the country and one of its leading spectator sports.

Despite its rapid spread, horse race betting has suffered severely from the recent rise of lotteries and other faster and simpler forms of gambling. From 1990 to 1997, daily average attendance at racetracks dropped 24 percent, from 4,610 to 3,499.[1] Although off-track and simulcast betting[2]—both of which allow gamblers to wager on a horse without being present for the race—have been legalized in all but a few pari-mutuel states, the total amount of money wagered on horse racing shrank from $22 billion in 1975 to $14 billion in 1997.[3] As a result, revenues to state and local governments from horse racing declined from $780 million in 1975 to $422 million in 1997. Even with shortened racing seasons, tracks continue to go out of business, including the fabled Roosevelt Raceway harness track in New York and the Hialeah thoroughbred track in Florida.[4] Many track owners now argue that unless they are allowed to offer casino games, they will have to shut down. Several states, including Delaware, Rhode Island, South Carolina, and West Virginia, have recently authorized tracks to install slot-machine-style electronic gaming devices.[5]

Similar stories can be told about pari-mutuel betting on greyhound racing, which, beginning in the 1920s, spread to more than sixty tracks in fifteen states, and jai alai, a Latin American game that has operated since the 1950s in Florida and, on occasion, in Connecticut and Rhode Island. Like horse racetracks, greyhound tracks and jai alai frontons have been hurt by competition from lotteries and other forms of gambling. The 1992 opening of the Foxwoods Resort and Casino in Connecticut, for example, drove all but one New England jai alai fronton out of business. Fourteen greyhound tracks shut down during the 1990s, leaving only forty-nine tracks in operation. Revenues to state governments from these forms of pari-mutuel betting have declined severely. In the fight to survive, greyhound tracks have followed the horse racing industry in persuading state governments to allow them to offer off-track betting, simulcast wagering, and, in some cases, on-site electronic gaming devices.

Charitable gambling also was widespread before the recent rise of commercial casinos. Bingo, raffles, pull tabs, "Las Vegas nights," and other games operated by or on behalf of religious, fraternal, and charitable organizations spread rapidly among the states during the 1950s. Unlike pari-mutuel betting, charitable gambling has remained reasonably successful ever since. Charitable bingo, for example, is legal in every state but Arkansas, Hawaii, Tennessee, and Utah. Not every state compiles data on charitable gambling, but by all accounts it is growing. Part of its political advantage over other forms of gambling is that it purports to offer bettors a chance to gamble for a good cause. Public opinion surveys consistently show that charitable bingo is the most widely supported form of gambling, with approval ratings exceeding 70 percent.[6] But legitimate concerns sometimes are voiced about the small amount of the money wagered (often less than 10 percent) that actually goes to charity, especially when charitable organizations contract with professional operators to conduct games on their behalf.[7]

The primacy of commercial casinos among the state-sanctioned forms of gambling is a phenomenon of the late 1980s and 1990s. From 1931 to 1975, Nevada was the only state to authorize casino gambling. New Jersey legalized casinos in Atlantic City in 1976. Its decision sparked a decade of similar efforts in nearly twenty other states, but until 1988 none of these efforts were successful. From 1988 to 2000, however, the ranks of commercial casino states more than quintupled, from two to eleven.

Although commercial casino gambling is legal in fewer states than are other forms of state-sanctioned gambling, it is a much more powerful presence in American life. Dollars tell part of the tale: in 1998, commercial casinos earned $22 billion, more than 40 percent of all the profits and revenues received by gambling businesses, charitable organizations, and governments that year. Jobs tell another part. The casino industry employs around 300,000 people, which is half of all those employed in legal gambling enterprises. The rest of the story is more disturbing, however. Casino gambling is regarded by some as the leading source of gambling disorders.

In this chapter, we focus on the politics of commercial casinos. We begin by chronicling, then explaining, the rise of commercial casino gambling, especially during the 1990s. We discuss the issues that dominate the current politics of commercial casinos, both in the eleven states that have them and the thirty-nine states that do not. We conclude the chapter by offering recommendations concerning public policy toward commercial casinos. Other forms of state-sanctioned gambling enter the story primarily in terms of how they have been affected by casino gambling. So do tribal casinos, although we suspend most of our discussion of this phenomenon until the next chapter.

THE RISE OF COMMERCIAL CASINOS

Nine of the eleven states that sanction commercial casino gambling made the decision to do so between 1988 and 1996. Yet the politics of their decisions cannot be understood apart from the much earlier experiences of their predecessors in casino gambling: Nevada, which legalized casinos in 1931, and New Jersey, which legalized them in 1976.

NEVADA

Nevada was one of many states to embrace state-sanctioned gambling in the 1930s as a strategy to raise revenue, but it was the only one to legalize commercial casinos. The Great Depression had increased state governments' funding needs while decreasing their traditional revenue sources. Because Nevada's population was too small and dispersed to make racetracks economically viable, and because its tradition of saloon-style gambling halls was even stronger than that of most other frontier states, it legalized commercial casinos rather than pari-mutuel betting. Organized crime, which lost its major source of revenue when Prohibition was repealed in 1933, gradually moved into the casino business. In 1966, seeking a cleaner image, Nevada warmly welcomed aeronautics multimillionaire Howard Hughes into the market. Three years later, after the federal government sued on antitrust grounds to prevent Hughes from buying more casinos, the state enacted the Corporate Gaming Act. The act allowed publicly traded corporations answerable to the Securities and Exchange Commission to own and operate casinos. A remarkable period of expansion ensued, led by companies such as Hilton, Hyatt, Holiday Inn, and Metro-Goldwyn-Mayer. By 1997, 429 commercial casinos were operating in Nevada. Nearly half of them were in Las Vegas, as were eleven of the twelve largest hotels in the country.

Over the years, Nevada's experience with commercial casinos conveyed four important lessons to other states that were thinking of legalizing this form of gambling. The first was that many Americans wanted to gamble on casino games. The second was that casinos could be the nucleus of resort complexes that would attract tourists for entertainment, recreation, and shopping as well as for gambling. Third, social problems spawned by gambling were a major casino-related concern. These problems included the gambling disorders that casino games help to provoke in some people and the proliferation of robbery, extortion, loan sharking, prostitution, and other forms of street crime that casino gambling sometimes stimulated and that local governments were left to deal with. The involvement of organized crime in the ownership of Nevada casinos, although largely ended by the time other states began to consider casino legislation, continued to shape the public's image of casinos. Finally, casinos required some amount of state supervision. Nevada developed a model for casino licensing and regulation that was intended to foster economic success and honest operations. The "Nevada model" treats casinos as corporate citizens that require close regulatory scrutiny to ensure the integrity of the games and keep out organized crime but that also have much to contribute in the way of jobs, capital investment, and tax revenues.[8]

NEW JERSEY

Nevada's decision to legalize commercial casino gambling did not trigger similar efforts in other states. In contrast, New Jersey's decision to do so sparked many state legalization campaigns. A pattern of casino politics emerged following New Jersey's legalization that prevailed during the late 1970s and 1980s. One aspect of that pattern was that, unlike in Nevada, proposals to legalize casinos henceforth would confine casino gambling to defined areas within a state, usually cities or regions that were economically distressed or that historically had been resort areas. Part of the explanation for the failure of a 1974 casino legalization effort in New Jersey was that it would have permitted casino gambling anywhere in the state. In contrast, the successful 1976 effort restricted casinos to Atlantic City.

A second aspect of casino politics that emerged from New Jersey was that proposals for casinos invariably would involve private ownership and state regulation. Another reason the state's 1974 effort had failed was that it proposed government-owned casinos, which many feared would place millions of dollars of public funds at risk in an uncertain business venture.[9] When New Jersey did legalize privately owned casinos two years later, it took a more stringent regulatory approach than Nevada. The "New Jersey model" regards commercial casinos as businesses that, although capable of contributing to the statewide and local economies, must be strictly regulated in number, location, and practices lest they endanger the public welfare.[10]

The third New Jersey–inspired aspect of the pattern of casino politics that subsequently prevailed during the late 1970s and 1980s was that public debates over casino legalization invariably came down to two competing campaign frames. Opponents would try to equate casinos with crime, while proponents would center their arguments on economics: jobs, tourism, capital investment, tax revenues to state and local government, and the fear that nearby states would reap these benefits by legalizing casinos first.

Fourth, starting with New Jersey, the role of the governor and other political, media, and business leaders became crucial in determining the outcome of casino legalization campaigns. Governor Brendan Byrne's fervent campaign for casinos in Atlantic City would turn out to be as unusual as it was important.

Finally, as in New Jersey, proposals to legalize casinos in the late 1970s and 1980s usually ended up on state ballots, either because the state constitution needed to be amended to allow casino gambling, with final approval requiring a voter referendum, or because casino proponents were seeking legalization through the initiative process.[11] New Jersey voters, who had defeated the 1974 casino proposal by a three-to-two margin, approved casino gambling by 56 percent to 44 percent in 1976.

The wave of legalization efforts that New Jersey's enactment of casino gambling sparked in other states was accompanied by widespread predictions that the same political and economic forces that were prompting states to create lotteries also would lead them to authorize commercial casinos.[12] In every case, these efforts called for state-regulated, privately owned casinos in either distressed urban areas such as Detroit, Michigan, and Bridgeport, Connecticut, or declining resort areas such as Miami Beach, Florida, New York's Catskill Mountains, and Hot Springs, Arkansas. Proponents in every state stressed the economic benefits of casino gambling and raised the specter of neighboring states acting first and snatching all of these promised benefits away.

CASINO LEGALIZATION CAMPAIGNS, 1978–88

Almost without exception, efforts to legalize commercial casino gambling in the aftermath of New Jersey doing so were unsuccessful. From 1978 to 1988, sixteen of seventeen casino campaigns failed in a total of twelve states: Florida (1978, 1982–84, 1986), Massachusetts

(1978–82), Connecticut (1979–83), New York (1977–84), New Hampshire (1979–80), Pennsylvania (1977–84), Michigan (1976–81, 1988), Texas (1984), Arkansas (1984), Colorado (1982, 1984), Louisiana (1986–88), and Ohio (1988).[13] Only one state, South Dakota in 1988, decided to legalize casinos, and it did so on a small-stakes basis as a strategy of historic preservation for the frontier town of Deadwood.

Casino opponents prevailed during this decade by rousing fears about crime more successfully than proponents were able to sell the purported economic benefits of casinos. They also raised doubts about the economic burden that casino gambling might place on the more family-oriented tourism industry and on efforts to attract new nongambling businesses. In nearly every state, the governor and most other leaders in the political, economic, and media spheres opposed casino legislation. Because of widespread business opposition, campaigns against casinos typically were well funded. In some cases the existing gambling establishments in a state, usually racetracks, spent heavily to defeat casino gambling. Casino companies themselves seldom got involved in state campaigns during the late 1970s and 1980s, and when they did they were not always supportive. For example, Resorts International, which had promoted Florida's first casino campaign in 1978, opposed the state's 1986 legalization effort because it regarded casino gambling in Miami as a threat to its new casinos in the Bahamas and the Caribbean.

CASINO LEGALIZATION CAMPAIGNS, 1989–96

Despite this long string of defeats, the tide began to turn in favor of commercial casinos at the end of the 1980s. The Supreme Court's 1987 decision in *California v. Cabazon Band of Mission Indians*[14] and Congress's passage of the Indian Gaming Regulatory Act (IGRA) in 1988 opened the door to casino gambling on many American Indian reservations, mostly in the Midwest and West. In some states, the seeming inevitability of tribal casinos made commercial casinos politically more palatable.[15] In addition, the Reagan and Bush administrations' cutbacks in federal spending on grant programs to the states, joined with a recession in the early 1990s and continuing public resistance to tax increases, heightened state officials' interest in finding new sources of revenue and economic development. Lotteries were the most popular palliative that many states embraced, but casinos were another. Consequently, the traditional resistance of governors to casino gambling, which had been so influential during the 1970s and 1980s, was softened in some states. In the early 1990s, Nevada loosened and then repealed a law that restricted Nevada-licensed companies from operating gambling enterprises in other states, which gave these companies an incentive to pursue casino legalization across the country. Finally, once one or two new states legalized casinos, or seemed likely to do so, the political pressure to legalize them in nearby states grew.

Commercial casinos spread most widely during the early 1990s among a far-flung group of states whose common denominator was the Mississippi River. As the map in Figure 3.1 makes plain, five of the eight states that have legalized commercial casinos since 1989 are Mississippi River states: Iowa, Illinois, Mississippi, Louisiana, and Missouri.[16] All of these states abandoned or deemphasized the land-based model of casino gambling in favor of water-based casinos.

In 1989, Iowa became the first state to legalize casinos on riverboats. Its reasons for doing so were varied. Tribal casinos were about to open in neighboring Minnesota and Wisconsin, which meant that Iowa was going to feel the effects of casino gambling no matter what it did. The farm equipment manufacturing industry in Bettendorf and Davenport, two small Iowa cities on the Mississippi River, was severely depressed. The romantic lore of the nineteenth-century riverboat gambler made water-based casinos seem more palatable to midwesterners than images of land-based casinos in Nevada and Atlantic City were. "We're selling the lore of Mark Twain," said the Iowa legislature's leading casino advocate.[17] Also contributing to the acceptability of water-based casinos was the requirement that gambling could only take place when the boats were actually cruising, with loss limits of $5 per bet and $200 per cruise. Iowa taxed casinos on a steeply rising scale that peaked at 20 percent of all gambling revenues above $3 million per year.

Casino gambling cascaded along the river in a pattern well described by the National Gambling Impact Study Commission (NGISC). "Riverboat casinos seemed to be the ideal instrument for delivering the budgetary nirvana," the NGISC's 1999 report concluded. "When located on the borders of other states, often conveniently near population centers across the river, they could be assured of drawing at least some of their revenues (and thus tax receipts) from the population of their benighted neighbors." Not unintentionally,

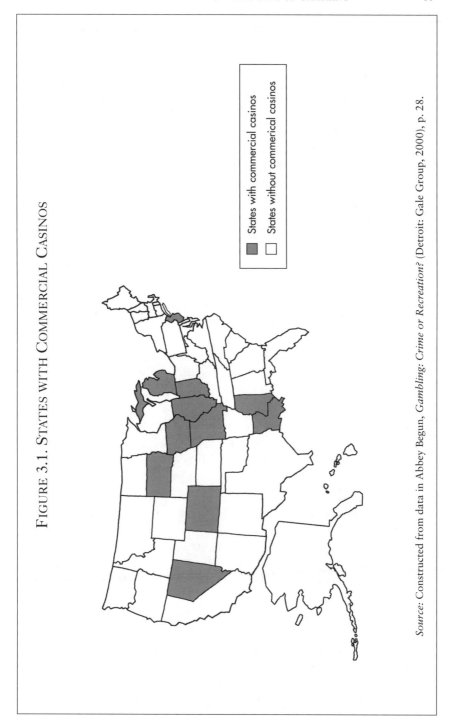

FIGURE 3.1. STATES WITH COMMERCIAL CASINOS

States with commercial casinos

States without commerical casinos

Source: Constructed from data in Abbey Begun, *Gambling: Crime or Recreation?* (Detroit: Gale Group, 2000), p. 28.

Iowa's casinos were located adjacent to Illinois and within striking distance of Chicago.

"Unfortunately . . . ," the report continues, "public officials in the targeted states quickly retaliated with riverboats of their own in the name of 'recapturing' the revenues of their wayward citizens."[18] Thus Illinois, a year after Iowa, legalized riverboat casinos in some of its depressed river cities, all of them closer to Chicago than Iowa's casinos were—and with none of the betting limits that drove off high-stakes gamblers, the casino industry's most highly prized clients. Indiana, whose declining industrial city of Gary is even closer to Chicago, followed suit in 1993 with water-based casinos on Lake Michigan and the Ohio River. Belatedly, Iowa abandoned its betting limits and allowed its casinos to remain docked rather than having to cruise.

In 1990, Mississippi, further south along the river that bears its name and with a stronger cultural claim to the riverboat gambling mythos, legalized commercial casinos in its long-depressed river counties and on the Gulf Coast, which had suffered severely from natural disasters and cutbacks in federal defense spending. Hoping to lure casino companies, Mississippi kept gambling taxes low: 8 percent to the state and, at local option, no more than 4 percent to the county where a casino was located. It placed no ceiling on the number of casinos that could operate in the state, allowing the market to decide. In contrast to most of the other riverboat states, which were reluctant converts to commercial casino gambling and thus adopted the stringent New Jersey model of regulation, Mississippi created a hybrid of the New Jersey and Nevada models. It confined casinos to designated parts of the state and regulated them closely, but it also treated them as valued corporate citizens. Within a few years, Mississippi trailed only Nevada and New Jersey as a center of commercial casino gambling.

Louisiana legalized commercial casinos in 1991. It departed from neighboring Mississippi's example of unlimited licensing by deciding to allow only fifteen water-based casinos and, in New Orleans, one land-based casino that would be required to pay a minimum tax to the state of $100 million per year. In 1992, Missouri legalized riverboat casinos, with a $500 loss limit per visit. Overcoming a series of objections by its supreme court, the state amended its constitution in 1994 to make clear that slot machines were legal, then amended it again in 1998 to establish that casinos did not have to be in the river itself but could sit in adjacent basins that had been dug to float casino barges. Supporters of casino gambling fought the restrictions on slot machines by arguing that they cost the state treasury $30 million per year in lost revenues from gamblers who were taking their business to other states. They passed the 1998 "boats in moats" measure by persuading the voters that the state supreme court was being unfair to companies that had already built their casinos in good faith.

Missouri's series of decisions in favor of riverboat casinos was unusual in several ways.[19] One is that its constitution required that all three casino-related decisions go before the voters. In contrast, the constitutions of none of the other Mississippi River states required statewide voter approval in order for the legislature to legalize casinos. "If that had been the case [in Mississippi]," said one of the state's leading casino supporters, "it never would have passed."[20] Some states, such as Louisiana, did not even require that local referenda be held in the affected cities and counties before casinos could open for business.[21] Second, casino companies spent heavily to influence the pro-gambling campaigns in Missouri.[22] Finally, Missouri's embrace of gambling marked the crest of the casino tide. Since 1992, only one state has chosen to authorize commercial casino gambling. Michigan voters narrowly approved a 1996 ballot measure to allow three casinos in Detroit, a city whose downtown has long been distressed and that sits directly across the Detroit River from a major casino in Windsor, Ontario.

EXPLAINING THE RISE OF COMMERCIAL CASINOS

The rise of commercial casinos unfolded in two phases. The first began in the mid-1970s, when New Jersey enacted casino gambling. New Jersey's decision sparked similar efforts for legalization in nearly twenty other states in the period from 1978 to 1988. Only one of these efforts succeeded, in the small South Dakota city of Deadwood, but casino gambling secured a place on the national political agenda and on the agenda of many states.

The second, more prolific phase in the rise of commercial casinos began in 1989, when Iowa became the first state to legalize water-based gambling on the Mississippi River. By the mid-1990s, Illinois, Indiana, Mississippi, Louisiana, and Missouri had followed suit. In addition, Colorado legalized land-based casinos in three small cities in 1990 and Michigan authorized downtown casinos in Detroit in 1996.

As was the case with state lotteries, the rise of commercial casinos can be explained partly in terms of national political influences, but mostly as the result of decentralized policymaking at the state level.

NATIONAL POLITICAL INFLUENCES

The Constitution places fewer limits on the federal government's authority concerning state-sanctioned gambling than it does in matters of state-sponsored gambling, such as lotteries. The former is less closely tied to the sovereign right of state governments to raise revenues to fund their activities.

In some cases, Congress has chosen to exercise its authority over state-sanctioned gambling. Congressional investigations of organized crime's role in the gambling industry, especially the televised hearings of the Kefauver Committee, spurred the enactment of the 1951 Gaming Devices Act, which prohibits the transportation of illegal gambling devices across state lines. The Racketeering Influenced and Corrupt Organization (RICO) statutes of the early 1970s also were aimed in part at weeding organized crime out of gambling. The Bank Secrecy Act of 1985 and the Money Laundering Control Act of 1986 targeted casinos and other cash-intensive businesses in an effort to prevent criminals from exchanging illegally obtained cash for untainted currency.[23] Taken together, these acts helped to speed the transition of the casino industry from its unsavory early years to its currently respectable status in the publicly traded corporate sector.

Other federal legislation has been less consistent in purpose. In 1992, for example, Congress passed the U.S. Flag Cruise Ship Competitiveness Act, which legalized gambling on American flag vessels in international waters. Two years later, it forbade gambling on international flights. Over the years, Congress turned the Federal Communications Act of 1934, which banned gambling advertising on radio and television broadcasts, into a Swiss cheese of exceptions that allows ads for tribal casinos, state lotteries, charitable gambling, and horse racing. Commercial casinos could broadcast ads for their restaurant, hotel, and entertainment venues, but not for their games.[24] In 1999, the Supreme Court removed even this prohibition in *Greater New Orleans Broadcasting Association v. United States* as an unconstitutional ban on commercial speech about a legal activity.[25]

On the whole, however, the federal government has chosen to defer to the states in the area of commercial casino gambling.[26] Its most important actions in this area have been inadvertent. The 1987 *Cabazon* decision by the Supreme Court and the passage of IGRA by Congress in 1988 were both concerned with tribal gambling. But, as noted above, the presence of tribal casinos in Minnesota and Wisconsin helped to set in motion the train of events that led Iowa, followed by other Mississippi River states, to legalize commercial casinos during the half decade that followed. Commercial casino gambling was more squarely addressed by the federal government in 1994, when President Bill Clinton considered taxing gambling revenues at 4 percent to help finance his welfare reform plan. Nothing came of this idea, but at the urging of members concerned about the rapid spread of legalized gambling, Congress voted in 1996 to create the National Gambling Impact Study Commission.

Clinton's "sin tax" proposal had one tangible effect: it provoked the casino industry—not just commercial casino corporations but also casino equipment manufacturers, suppliers, and vendors—to form the American Gaming Association (AGA). The AGA, a Washington-based trade association that is headed by former Republican National Committee chair Frank Fahrenkopf, uses both "insider" (lobbying and campaign contributions) and "outsider" (public advocacy) strategies of political influence on behalf of its members.[27] Among its victories, the AGA persuaded Congress to limit the NGISC's subpoena powers,[28] influenced the selection of commission members to include casino advocates as well as opponents, and stymied congressional efforts to repeal the wagering loss deduction that allows bettors to pay federal income tax on net rather than gross winnings. In the six years following the AGA's formation in 1994, the commercial casino industry donated $16 million to the national Republican and Democratic parties, nearly triple the $6 million it had donated during the previous six years.[29]

In contrast, the AGA's main adversary among national interest groups, the National Coalition Against Legalized Gambling (NCALG), is based in Galena, Illinois. Although NCALG makes the most of its meager financial resources to rouse public concerns about gambling and, with particular effectiveness, to assist casino opponents in the states, the organization's lobbying efforts in Washington are limited.[30]

Both NCALG (1994) and the AGA (1995) were formed after most of the commercial casino states had made their decisions for legalization. The national climate of opinion, however, was already undergoing some changes. In general, the antitax mood that prevailed during the late 1980s and early 1990s led hard-pressed state governments to place a premium on sources of revenue other than taxes. In particular, public opinion polls, while revealing continuing concern about casinos' effects on crime and social problems, found an increase in overall support for "casino gambling at resort areas" (from 54 percent in 1992 to 68 percent in 1996), "casino gambling on so-called 'river boats'" (from 60 percent in 1992 to 63 percent in 1996), and "casino gambling in a major city" (from 40 percent in 1992 to 55 percent in 1996).[31]

Expert opinion on casino gambling was much more divided, but with subtle changes over time that have worked in the casinos' favor. Neither the 1976 report of the Commission on the Review of the National Policy toward Gambling nor the 1999 NGISC report were avowedly for or against commercial casinos. But the 1976 report focused its attention on casinos and organized crime, the last subject the casino industry ever wants at the center of public discussion. The 1999 report, although concerned and at times critical of casinos' social consequences, found little evidence that organized crime remained a problem and noted that it had received considerable testimony about the economic benefits of commercial casinos—exactly the subject the industry most wants to be discussed.

DECENTRALIZED POLICYMAKING

As with lotteries, so with commercial casinos: national political influences have shaped the context of policymaking, but the states have made most of the actual policies. Processes of policy diffusion have been at work in some states, as has the influence of the states' internal characteristics.

Diffusion. Policy diffusion occurs in two main ways. One, which we call *ordinary diffusion,* is when a state adopts a solution out of admiration for the approach that another state has developed to a problem that both states share. The other—the way of *reactive diffusion*—is the process in which a state copies a policy from another state in an effort to fend off the unwanted consequences of that state's policy. Reactive diffusion has been the more common of the two in state policymaking concerning commercial casinos.[32]

Ordinary diffusion was at work in four of the ten states that have legalized commercial casino gambling during the past quarter century. New Jersey was inspired in part by the example of Nevada, which had shown that casinos operated by publicly traded corporations could generate capital investment, jobs, tourism, and substantial revenues for the state treasury without involving organized crime.[33] South Dakota took its cue from New Jersey's decision to use casinos as a strategy of economic recovery for a distressed city. Colorado, in turn, followed South Dakota's example in some of its fading mining towns. Mississippi learned the possibilities of water-based casinos from Iowa. It embraced some components of Nevada's model of casino regulation so thoroughly that for a time its legalization bill mistakenly included references to Nevada rather than Mississippi in paragraphs that had been copied in full from Nevada's gambling statutes.

The other six states that have legalized commercial casinos did so reactively, as a strategy to keep their people's gambling dollars from flowing into neighboring states. Iowa adopted casino gambling in the certain knowledge that tribal casinos were about to open in neighboring Minnesota and Wisconsin. Illinois legalized casinos to keep its bettors from going to Iowa, and Indiana followed suit to protect itself against Illinois. Farther south, casino gambling in Mississippi placed Louisiana and Missouri on the defensive. Both states legalized commercial casinos within two years of Mississippi's decision to do so. Michigan authorized commercial casinos in Detroit less than a year after casino gambling began in adjacent Windsor, Ontario. The politics of reactive diffusion also spurred casino legalization campaigns, thus far unsuccessful, in a host of other states, including three of Mississippi's neighbors (Arkansas, Alabama, and Tennessee) and two of New Jersey's (Pennsylvania and New York).

Internal characteristics. In addition to the processes of policy diffusion, the internal characteristics of states have had a great deal to do with whether or not they have chosen to legalize casino gambling. In *The Last Resort*, their landmark work on the politics of casino gambling in the 1970s and 1980s, John Dombrink and William Thompson focused exclusively on internal state characteristics.[34] With Nevada and New Jersey as the only casino states in the country, policy diffusion across state lines was a negligible and thus an easily overlooked part of the process. In its absence, the authors concluded that a number of internal characteristics influenced the likelihood that a state would allow casinos to operate within its borders: *political environment* factors such as the economy and the state's prior experience with gambling;[35] *political elite and active interests* factors, including the positions of public officials and business interests on casinos; *campaign sponsorship* factors such as the credibility and financial commitment of casino advocates; and *campaign issue dominance* factors, notably the ability of casino supporters to frame the public debate as being about economic development rather than crime, morality, or quality of life. The politics of lotteries, Dombrink and Thompson found, could be accounted for by a "gravity model"— that is, if these four factors were, on balance, more positive than negative, a state would enact a lottery. Because casinos were more controversial, however, a "veto model" was necessary to explain the politics of casino legalization. If even one of the four factors was averse to a casino measure, the measure would fail.

Dombrink and Thompson's veto model accounted very well for the failure of casino legalization campaigns in every state but New Jersey from the 1970s through the late 1980s, when their research was concluded. The model did not foretell the events of the following decade, however, when the ranks of commercial casino states increased from two to eleven. Clearly some new developments occurred in this period that were politically relevant. For example, as Thompson himself later pointed out, Nevada's loosening and then abandonment of restrictions on out-of-state investments by casino companies during the early 1990s freed those companies to lobby for casino legalization around the country.[36] In addition, once enough states had legalized commercial casinos to form a critical mass, the workings of ordinary and reactive policy diffusion came into play.

More important than these new developments was an internal state characteristic that usually is overlooked by students of state politics and policymaking: the varying influence of state constitutions. Legalization campaigns during the past quarter century almost always have entailed amending the state constitution, a process that in most states requires both legislative enactment and voter approval in a referendum. One of the reasons that casino legalization efforts failed in nearly every instance during the 1970s and 1980s is that they either were defeated at the polls or never reached the ballot because legislators were certain that they would be defeated. Indeed, two of Dombrink and Thompson's four clusters of politically meaningful factors in casino campaigns—"campaign sponsorship" and "campaign issue dominance"—pertain to referenda. As it happens, these two clusters tended in many states to be more adverse to casino efforts than the "political environment" and "political elite and active interests" factors.[37]

Beginning with Iowa, efforts to expand commercial casino gambling became more focused on states whose constitutions did not ban casinos or whose amendment processes did not require approval by the voters.[38] From 1989 to 1993, five of the seven states that legalized casinos did so by vote of the legislature, without any statewide referendum: Iowa, Illinois, Mississippi, Louisiana, and Indiana. (The exceptions were South Dakota and Missouri.) Not surprisingly, the dramatic slowdown in casino legalizations that began in 1994 coincided with the reemergence of casino campaigns in states that require a referendum, such as Ohio, Florida, and Arkansas. In truth, not many states are left whose constitutions would allow commercial casinos to be legalized without the voters' approval.

THE CONTEMPORARY POLITICS OF COMMERCIAL CASINOS AND OTHER FORMS OF GAMBLING

The casino juggernaut ran strongly during a brief period beginning in the late 1980s, but has lost momentum since then. From 1994 to 2000, efforts to legalize commercial casinos were successful in Missouri and Michigan. But they were defeated everywhere else. Ballot measures to authorize casino gambling failed, usually by margins of twenty percentage points or more, in Florida, Colorado, and Rhode Island in 1994, in Ohio, Arkansas, and Colorado in 1996, and in Arkansas again in 2000. Lobbying campaigns to persuade state legislatures to legalize commercial casinos have failed in Alabama, Connecticut, Kansas, Maryland, New York, Pennsylvania, Tennessee, Virginia, and West Virginia.[39] Only tribal casinos, which are the subject of Chapter 4, have fared reasonably well at the polls in recent elections. Arizona voters instructed their governor to reverse his policy of refusing to negotiate further casino compacts with American Indian tribes in 1996, and, in both 1998 and 2000, California passed propositions to give tribes within its borders exclusive authority to offer casino gambling.

In the meantime, other gambling enterprises have been beseeching state governments for the right to broaden their offerings. Arkansas's failed 1996 casino ballot measure was primarily an effort to allow the Oaklawn horse racetrack to open a casino; the unsuccessful 2000 initiative would have added to the roster of authorized casinos the state's other pari-mutuel betting site, the greyhound racetrack located across the Tennessee state line from Memphis.[40] Tracks also have sought permission to install slot-machine-style electronic gaming devices. During the 1990s, they were successful in five small states but unsuccessful in at least twelve others, including Maine in 2000. Tracks have done better in their current quest to expand account wagering in "closed-door subscriber-based" systems. Nine states, including New York, Ohio, Pennsylvania, and Kentucky, now allow gamblers to bet on races by phone or online.

As is the case with lotteries, the contemporary politics of commercial casinos differs in casino and noncasino states. In the thirty-nine states that do not allow commercial casino gambling, the main issue is whether to legalize casinos or not. Complicating this issue, many of these states already have tribal casinos operating within their borders. For the eleven states with commercial casinos, the important issues involve regulation, taxation, operations, and expansion, along with crime and other social consequences.

STATES WITHOUT COMMERCIAL CASINOS

In most of the thirty-nine states without commercial casinos a combination of political forces is at work, some of them making states more likely to legalize casinos and others making them less likely to do so. Some political forces, such as public opinion, cut both ways. A Gallup poll taken in April and May of 1999, for example, asked a national sample: "When casinos open in a community, do you feel that it helps or hurts the community's economy?" An identically phrased question was asked about casinos' effect on "everyday family and community life." By 67 percent to 23 percent, respondents said casinos help the local economy. By 56 percent to 24 percent, they said casinos hurt family and community life.[41]

Forces in Favor of Legalization. One important political force that in some states favors commercial casino legalization efforts is the policy of neighboring states. When casinos are available next door, the case for legalization becomes politically more persuasive. Many citizens of a noncasino state are going to drive across the state line to gamble anyway, the argument goes, so why not legalize casinos, which will pay taxes at home? Although policy diffusion has occurred less consistently with casinos than with lotteries (for example, no state bordering on New Jersey or Nevada has legalized commercial casinos), most of the states that now allow casino gambling are Mississippi River states that were following the lead of their neighbors. Moreover, several states that frequently return to the casino issue, such as Arkansas, Ohio, and North Dakota, share a border with one or more states that allow commercial casinos.

A second pro-casino political force at work today is the money that casino interests have poured into state and national political coffers. In July 1999, the General Accounting Office reported that political contributions from gambling interests to federal candidates and national party committees had risen from $1.1 million in 1992, a presidential election year, to $5.7 million in 1998, a midterm election year. (Democrats received more in some elections, Republicans in others.) During this same period, the number of federal candidates receiving gambling-related campaign contributions rose from 146 to 269. By 1998, the gambling industry ranked thirty-seventh among ninety-two industry and interest groups in federal campaign contributions.[42] At the state level, more than $100 million in political donations and lobbying fees were spent to influence legislators between 1994 and 1996 alone. For example, gambling companies spent $11.5 million in a successful 1994 effort to amend Missouri's constitution so that casinos could offer slot machines.[43]

A third contemporary political force that works to the benefit of commercial casino legalization is an indirect and unintended result of the NGISC. Congress created this commission at the behest of gambling opponents. But the commissioners heard laudatory testimony about the economic benefits of casinos from the elected leaders of Elgin, Illinois, Bettendorf, Iowa, Tunica, Mississippi, and other casino locales. Although not uncritical of casino gambling's effects on communities, the NGISC's public hearings and final report drew attention to casinos' economic benefits and away from the old notion that all casino towns are like Las Vegas and Reno used to be— hotbeds of corruption and seediness. As a result of the NGISC, states that are now considering legalizing commercial casinos have many examples, apparently government certified, to emulate. This is especially the case for states with counties or regions in which other industries are scarce. For example, proposals for casino gambling as a strategy to revive the Miami tourism industry periodically appear on

Florida's policy agenda. The prosperity of the 1990s muted such proposals in most states, but they may return in tougher economic times.

An additional economic argument in favor of casino legalization
is grounded in a study that the NGISC commissioned from the
University of Chicago's National Opinion Research Council (NORC).
NORC conducted a quantitative analysis of one hundred communities from 1980 to 1996. Communities within fifty miles of a casino
experienced a statistically significant positive effect on four of five
employment measures and on seven of sixteen income-earning measures. Even when a community's net personal income did not increase,
NORC found, income from employment rose in proportion to income
from welfare payments.[44]

The pleas of economically depressed areas for casinos are politically more persuasive when these areas are located near "feeder
markets"—that is, population centers that contain many would-be
customers. Certain counties in which the casino industry has thrived
have experienced a dramatic turnaround in the past decade thanks to
the presence of a large feeder market, as Tunica, Mississippi, has
from nearby Memphis. In contrast, other casino sites—for example,
Greenville, Mississippi, and Joliet, Illinois—are situated far from feeder markets. To the extent that their casinos prosper, they do so by
draining dollars from the local economy.

States without commercial casinos also feel pressures to allow racetracks and bingo halls to offer casino-style slot machines and table
games. Every state but Hawaii, Tennessee, and Utah has some form of
gambling and therefore some industry that is interested in competing for
gambling dollars. A common argument from the horse racing industry,
for example, is that tracks simply cannot compete with commercial casinos in neighboring states. Some states have responded to this argument
by allowing slots and video poker at horse and dog tracks. Bettors at
these tracks face a bevy of gambling options as varied as the choices
available to hungry shoppers in the food court of any mall in America.

The final pro-casino political force at work in states without
commercial casinos consists of groups that would like to benefit
directly from taxes on gambling. When casino gambling appears on
a state's policy agenda, the age-old saying that "politics makes strange
bedfellows" often becomes apt. Teachers, whose pension funds may
receive money from taxes on the casino industry, or senior citizens,
whose services may be expanded from such revenues, may align themselves with more traditional casino supporters.

Forces against Legalization. Despite this long list of pro-casino political forces, the forces that currently are arrayed against casino legalization, taken together, tend to outweigh them in nearly every noncasino state. First, and perhaps foremost, almost every state is benefiting from a number of economic and political trends that have reduced the pressures to legalize casino gambling as a new revenue source. State coffers have been swollen in recent years by the increased tax receipts and reduced demands for spending brought about by a booming economy, recent federal policies such as welfare reform and increased spending on grant programs for states and localities, and the substantial funds that states are receiving as part of their legal settlement with the tobacco companies.

Antigambling casino groups are a second political force working against legalization. Although NCALG is heavily outgunned in Washington, it can be counted on to enter any state casino legalization campaign. NCALG brings organizational skill and an array of anticasino arguments to the task of helping to mobilize local opponents. Among officeholders, governors and state law enforcement officials often campaign against casino legalization proposals, as George Voinovich did in Ohio in 1996 and Mike Huckabee did in Arkansas in 2000. In addition, some of the fiercest opposition to new casinos has come from the owners and operators of existing gambling establishments, especially charitable bingo halls and racetracks that see no prospect of being allowed to offer casino games themselves. These establishments often feel that they are fighting for their existence.

Organizations such as NCALG are quick to point out that gambling disorders are spreading in the United States and to argue that the states should do nothing to aggravate this problem. The NGISC estimated that 7.5 million American adults and 7.9 million American adolescents are problem or pathological gamblers. Although definitions of these terms vary, the NGISC noted that all researchers agree that pathological gamblers "engage in destructive behaviors: they commit crimes, they run up large debts, they damage relationships with family and friends, and they kill themselves." Problem gamblers also suffer a wide range of adverse consequences from their gambling, but fall below the threshold of at least five of the ten American Psychiatric Association criteria for addiction, the standard the NGISC used to define pathological gambling. These criteria include "repeated unsuccessful attempts to control, cut back, or stop gambling" and "illegal acts such as forgery, fraud, theft, or embezzlement to finance gambling."[45] Because the frequency of gambling disorders increases (often doubles) in most areas that legalize casinos,[46] anticasino groups point to the social consequences of casino gambling, such as theft and damaged or abusive relationships, as an additional reason not to legalize it in the first place.

Third, not everyone accepts the argument that communities benefit from casinos. In addition to the one-hundred-community quantitative study that it conducted for the NGISC, NORC also did detailed case studies of ten casino communities. Leaders in six communities complained to NORC interviewers that the jobs casinos provided were mostly low paying or part-time without benefits. They also reported that the advent of casino gambling had triggered an increase in domestic violence. In six of the ten communities, at least one respondent claimed that child neglect rose after casinos opened. In some cases, children were left alone, at home or even in parking lots, while parents gambled. Critics of casino gambling argue that although the economic benefits of casinos may seem obvious, the costs are greater because local governments are left to deal with the economic ramifications of these social problems.[47]

Fourth on the list of contemporary anticasino political forces is the recent trial and conviction on casino-related corruption charges of former governor Edwin Edwards of Louisiana and of casino owner Eddie De Bartolo, Jr., which have reinforced old doubts about the susceptibility of commercial casino gambling to criminal influences. For years, the casino industry has worked hard to erase these doubts, and, despite widespread public perceptions of gangster domination, reinforced by movies such as *The Godfather* and *Casino*, the industry has met with considerable success. In 1986, for example, the President's Commission on Organized Crime decided not to issue a report on gambling because it no longer regarded casinos as being tied to organized crime. In recent years, financial analysts have treated commercial casinos as a legitimate and successful industry. However, the corruption in Louisiana has provided grist for the rhetorical mill of casino opponents, especially because De Bartolo had been a part of casino legalization efforts in several states, including Ohio, Oklahoma, and California.

A final aspect of the contemporary politics of casino gambling involves states without commercial casinos but with tribal casinos. Some states, such as New York, have considered legalizing commercial casinos because it seems to them, in view of the size and scope of many tribal casinos, that such a policy already exists in the state. In most states, however, the presence of tribal casinos has virtually put an end to discussions of commercial casino legalization. By assuring tribes that they will face no competition from commercial casinos, states such as Connecticut and California have been able to negotiate compacts that include generous payments from the tribes to the state treasury and other concessions. In any event, public opinion in states with tribal casinos often regards the addition of commercial casinos as introducing more gambling than the voters want. Some voters also are reluctant to enact a policy that might be perceived as hostile to Native Americans. Further, tribes with casinos are not without political resources of their own. Through campaign contributions and the hiring of lobbyists, they often are able to fight effectively against commercial competition.[48]

STATES WITH COMMERCIAL CASINOS

Once a state decides to legalize commercial casinos, a host of subsidiary questions arises. Among the first is whether casinos should be regulated according to the Nevada model, the somewhat stricter New Jersey model, or some combination of the two. As mentioned above, the Nevada model specifies that the main goal of legalizing casinos is to maximize their economic benefits for the state and its citizens. These benefits include capital investment, jobs, tourism, and tax revenues. The model allows the market a relatively free hand in matters such as the number and location of casinos, but it places the state in a policing role to the extent necessary to ensure the integrity of the games and to keep out organized crime. The New Jersey model not only assigns the policing functions to the state but also imposes restrictions on matters such as where casinos may be located, the hours they may operate, the amount of money that individuals may bet, and the types of games casinos may offer. Regulatory policies in most commercial casino states more closely resemble the New Jersey model than the Nevada model.[49]

Other questions that must be addressed in commercial casino states include how much the state will tax slots, card games, and revenues from casino-related resort activities and how much cities and counties will be allowed to tax the industry. Currently, tax policies vary a great deal from state to state. Mississippi, for example, taxes casinos at 8 percent of gross revenues and allows localities to tax them an additional 4 percent. In contrast, Iowa taxes its most profitable casinos at a rate of 20 percent.

States also must decide whether to regulate the setting in which casino gambling takes place in order to discourage irresponsible and even dangerous levels of gambling. These decisions involve the presence of automated teller machines on casino floors, the distribution of free alcoholic drinks to bettors, the visibility of gambling to children who are staying with their families in casino hotels, and the extent to which casino companies are required to contribute to the study and treatment of gambling disorders.

Finally, when a state confines commercial casinos to a limited number of localities, pressures sometimes arise to legalize casino gambling in other parts of the state. Mississippi's 1990 Gaming Control Act, for example, permitted commercial casinos to operate in any of the eleven counties along the Mississippi River and in the three counties on the Gulf of Mexico, as long as the county's voters did not reject casino gambling in a referendum. Several years later, the mayor and city council of Jackson, the state's largest city and its capital, pressed the legislature to allow its voters to authorize commercial casino gambling. Des Moines made a similar push after Iowa legalized commercial casinos in some cities.

POLICY RECOMMENDATIONS

The scattered presence of commercial casinos across the American landscape reflects, perhaps as no other area of public policy does, the incredible variety of policies that can emerge from a decentralized, federal system of government. Utah seems as likely to authorize casino gambling as it is to legalize crack cocaine. Nevada seems as likely to expel casinos as it is to prohibit the sale and distribution of ice cream.

Somewhere between these two states that are equal and opposite in their resoluteness regarding casinos are many other states that either have chosen to open their doors cautiously to commercial casino gambling or have carefully considered doing so. We respect and appreciate the diversity of policies that exists among states regarding casinos. Citizens can and, if they so desire, should live far or near casinos based on their own preferences. Having said this, we do offer some specific recommendations to states without commercial casinos and to states with commercial casinos.

STATES WITHOUT COMMERCIAL CASINOS

In the chapter on state lotteries, we strongly urged states without lotteries not to legalize them in any form. We make no similarly sweeping recommendation to states without commercial casinos.

States that have severely depressed areas and share borders with casino states should consider with great care a policy of legalized commercial casinos. Voters should look skeptically on any proposal to legalize casino gambling that is not buttressed by solid research indicating that the benefits of commercial casinos will outweigh the costs. Their consideration of such a policy should be informed by lengthy public debates culminating in a statewide referendum. The issues raised in such debates should include but not be limited to the social and economic consequences of casino gambling, the presence or absence of tribal casinos in the state, the appropriate regulatory framework to be imposed on the casino industry, and the possibility that once casinos are legalized in limited areas of the state, other areas may clamor for legalization.

With one exception, our recommendations on these issues are either discussed in the next section or vary according to the situations faced by particular states. The exception is our recommendation that no state with tribal casinos should legalize commercial casinos. Presumably the tribal casinos were opened to give the Native American tribes whose lands are within a state a fighting chance to attain economic self-sufficiency. Introducing competition from commercial casinos would surely undermine their prospects for success.

We also recommend to states without commercial casinos that they do not let casinos in through the back door at racetracks. We share the NGISC commissioners' position that it is inappropriate for states to "allow the introduction of casino-style gambling into pari-mutuel facilities for the primary purpose of saving a pari-mutuel facility that the market has determined no longer serves the community or for the purpose of competing with other forms of gambling."[50] We extend that recommendation to cover other noncasino gambling sites, such as bingo halls.

STATES WITH COMMERCIAL CASINOS

Although we are less critical of casinos than of lotteries, we recognize that casinos pose dangers to a number of people that lotteries do not, especially casinos with high-stakes games and high-stimulation environments. But the benefits of job creation and economic development that commercial casinos can provide usually make them a more acceptable form of legalized gambling than lotteries. So does the absence of state sponsorship and, through advertising, state encouragement of gambling. Thus, we make fewer suggestions to states with commercial casinos than we did in Chapter 2 to states that run lotteries.

We favor an approach to casino regulation that in some ways more closely resembles the Nevada model than the New Jersey model. Having chosen to legalize casinos, states should regard them as tax-paying, job-creating corporate citizens, albeit ones that require special regulatory attention to ensure honest operations. If a state chooses to follow the New Jersey model of regulation rather than the Nevada model, it should at least not make the mistake of limiting the number of casino licenses. Such a limitation creates a scarce and valuable resource that can only be obtained from the state. The consequence is that the likelihood of public officials being corrupted rises dramatically. Louisiana's recent trial and conviction of former governor Edwards is ample evidence of that.

Second, lest the absence of a limit on the number of casinos lead to a casino on every street corner, we recommend that states mandate casino companies to match their investments in gambling facilities dollar-for-dollar with investments in land-based resort development: hotels, shops, restaurants, and other recreational facilities. Compared with allowing gambling halls alone, such a policy contributes more to the local economy by boosting tourism, generating substantial capital investments, and providing employment and managerial opportunities that are transferable beyond the casino industry.

Some casino companies will find this requirement to be financially untenable in many cities and counties because the only way they can make money is from local gamblers. That is reason enough to discourage them from opening a casino in the first place. Mississippi, for example, found a few years after it authorized casino gambling in its river and coastal areas that casinos in counties not located near population centers or along interstate highways were simply drawing on local residents for their business. The state decided to mandate that future casino construction would be governed by a dollar-for-dollar land investment requirement. Casino companies responded by electing not to open new gambling halls in counties where the prospects for tourist income were poor.

Our last and perhaps most important recommendation concerns the ways casinos contribute to gambling disorders. Casino corporations should stop talking out of both sides of their mouths on this issue. They are quick to point out that they spend money (and, to their credit, more money than anyone else) to study and treat gambling disorders and that they do not want to do anything that drives their best customers into bankruptcy. Meanwhile, they create an environment in which people have easy access to money that they may not be able to afford to lose. We recommend that casinos impose stricter guidelines on the lines of credit they extend to bettors and that cash advances on credit cards be disallowed on casino properties.

4

TRIBAL GAMBLING

As we have seen in Chapters 2 and 3, most of American politics and policymaking concerning gambling takes place in the states. In 1998, legal betting in the United States generated $54 billion in profits for businesses and revenues to governments. Of that amount, $46 billion—85 percent—was earned by gambling enterprises that are either owned (lotteries) or licensed by state governments, especially commercial casinos, racetracks, and charitable games.[1]

All of the remaining revenue from legal gambling—more than $8 billion in 1998, or 15 percent—is earned by American Indian tribes, mostly from casinos on tribal lands. Tribal gambling is by far the fastest-growing form of legal betting in the country. From 1988, when tribes earned $212 million from seventy gambling facilities in sixteen states, to 1998, when they earned $8.2 billion from 260 facilities in thirty-one states, tribal gambling revenues grew nearly forty-fold.[2] Casinos have displaced bingo halls as the leading source of tribal gambling revenues. California's passage of Proposition 1A in March 2000 will further accelerate this growth: Indian tribes now have exclusive authority to own casinos in that state.

The politics of tribal gambling is uniquely multisovereign and therefore uniquely complex. The role of the federal government, which holds American Indian lands in trust, has been of greatest consequence. The role of tribal governments, which are sovereign in their relationship to the states, also has been significant. State governments are less important actors, but their role has not been insubstantial.

In this chapter we begin by chronicling the spread of tribal gambling, then attempt to explain why that spread has occurred in terms of national, state, and (in this case) tribal political influences. We assess the current issues and controversies concerning the politics of tribal gambling. Finally, we offer policy recommendations to federal, state, and tribal governments.

THE RISE OF TRIBAL GAMBLING

The legal relationship between the federal government and American Indian tribes is, as Chief Justice John Marshall wrote in the 1831 Supreme Court case of *Cherokee Nation v. Georgia*, "unlike that of any other two people in history."[3] Marshall's opinion set in motion a long train of attempts by the Court to define this unique relationship. On the one hand, he wrote, a tribe is sovereign in the same way the federal and state governments are sovereign: it is a "distinct political society . . . capable of managing its own affairs and governing itself." On the other hand, a tribe is to the federal government like "a ward to his guardian"; that is, the relationship is one of fiduciary trust in which the federal government is empowered to make decisions for the tribe with the understanding that those decisions will be in the tribe's best interest. As Marshall wrote in the 1832 case of *Worcester v. Georgia*, a tribe is a "domestic dependent nation" in relation to the federal government and thus is free from state interference: "the laws of Georgia can have no force."[4] A more recent formulation by the Court of this complex set of relationships is that Congress has power "to control or manage Indian affairs" as long as that power is used for "appropriate measures for protecting and advancing the tribe."[5]

Over the years, the federal government has been an incompetent guardian at best, a venal one at worst. The ill treatment of tribes has ranged from stripping them of their historic lands—the same Cherokee Nation for which Marshall expressed concern was overrun by settlers from Georgia when President Andrew Jackson refused to enforce the *Worcester* decision—to policies verging on outright extermination. The effects of this abuse continue to be felt. Native Americans have some of the highest rates of poverty, unemployment, alcoholism, poor health, and incarceration of any group in the United States.[6]

Politically, however, attempts by Native Americans to expand tribal influence began to bear fruit in the late 1960s and early 1970s. The activist American Indian Movement, the litigation-focused

Native American Rights Fund, and other groups sought a greater measure of self-determination in tribal political and economic affairs. A combination of Republican presidents promoting a "New Federalism" that would devolve power from Washington to sub-national units of government and Democratic congresses that were sympathetic to the causes of ethnic and racial minorities responded positively to these demands.[7] In 1975, for example, Congress passed and President Gerald Ford signed the Indian Self-Determination and Education Assistance Act, which gave tribal governments consider-able discretion concerning how federal programs would be admin-istered on their reservations. During the 1980s, the Reagan administration concentrated its efforts on economic self-determination for American Indian tribes, partly out of concern for their well-being and partly in the hope that flourishing tribal economies would reduce their dependence on federal funds, which the administration severe-ly reduced in 1981.

Efforts by the federal government to promote tribal self-determination had sometimes been made prior to the 1970s.[8] That these efforts met with little success was hardly the tribes' fault. Federal attempts in the late nineteenth century to encourage farming, for example, were poorly matched to the barren soil on most Indian lands, and state and local governments often viewed tribal enterprises as a threat to established businesses.

In the late 1970s, however, at a time when state lotteries were proliferating, some tribes began to invest in gambling operations. The Seminole Tribe in Florida took the lead by opening a bingo hall with higher-stakes games than were permitted by the state in non-tribal bingo halls. After the state of Florida declined to challenge a federal circuit court ruling that authorized the Seminoles to operate their games,[9] tribes in Wisconsin, Connecticut, California, and other states followed suit. The Reagan administration lent its support to these efforts. The Departments of the Interior, Health and Human Services, and Housing and Urban Development all provided loans and other financial assistance to help tribes develop gambling facili-ties that could attract bettors from surrounding areas. By 1985, around one hundred tribes were sponsoring bingo games, some with jackpots of $100,000 or more.

Several state governments, alarmed that much more extensive gambling operations than they had authorized were operating within their borders, elected to fight these efforts. Constitutionally, however, they stood on weak ground. Although the relationship between federal sovereignty and tribal sovereignty may be complex, the relationship between state and tribal sovereignty is not. As the Supreme Court reiterated in the 1980 case of *Washington* v. *Confederated Colville Tribes*, unless the federal government chooses to allow states to apply their laws to Native Americans on reservations, "tribal sovereignty is dependent on, and subordinate to, only the Federal Government, not the States."[10] The federal government, far from wanting to help states stifle profit-making tribal gambling enterprises, was encouraging these enterprises.

In 1980, citing Public Law 280, a federal statute that empowers the states to enforce their criminal laws on tribal land, the state of California tried to shut down two bingo parlors and a card room operated by the Cabazon and Morongo Bands of Mission Indians on their reservations near Palm Springs. Rebuffed by the lower courts, California took its case to the Supreme Court. Nevada, Arizona, New Mexico, Washington, and Connecticut, most of which had significant tribal gambling operations within their borders, supported California with briefs of amici curiae. But in 1987, in a six-to-three decision that crossed ideological lines (for example, it placed Chief Justice William Rehnquist and Justice William Brennan on the tribes' side, and Justices John Paul Stevens and Antonin Scalia on the state's), the Court ruled in favor of the tribes in the case of *California* v. *Cabazon Band of Mission Indians*. In essence, the Court held that unless a state consistently treats gambling as either a crime or a violation of its constitution, it cannot forbid gambling on tribal lands. Because California offered a virtual cornucopia of legal gambling—not just bingo and card rooms but also a lottery and horse race betting—the Cabazons' gambling operations stood on solid legal ground.

Responding to concerns expressed by many states about organized crime possibly gaining a foothold in the burgeoning tribal bingo industry, as well as about efforts by some tribes to acquire land near cities to serve as new gambling enclaves, Congress had begun to consider legislation to regulate tribal gambling in the mid-1980s. The *Cabazon* ruling, which the states feared (and the tribes hoped) would deny the states any say about gambling on reservations, spurred it to action.

In 1988, Congress voted overwhelmingly (323 to 84 in the House, viva voce in the Senate) to enact the Indian Gaming Regulatory Act (IGRA) in order "to provide a statutory basis for the operation of gaming by Indian tribes as a means of promoting tribal economic development, self-sufficiency, and strong tribal governments." The law requires that any gambling facilities on tribal land be owned by the tribe as a whole, and that the revenues generated by these facilities be used primarily to fund tribal government operations and programs, the general welfare of the tribe and its members, and tribal economic development, including education, health, and improvements to infrastructure. IGRA defines tribal land as consisting for the most part of land the tribe owned at the time the act was passed. But it allows tribes to purchase and open gambling facilities on new land if the secretary of the interior and the governor of the state agree.

IGRA divided gambling on tribal lands into three classes, each of them regulated differently:

- *Class I gambling* consists of traditional tribal games and "social games" played for prizes of nominal value. Such gambling is legal on tribal lands and is regulated solely by each tribe.

- *Class II gambling* consists of card games that are not played against the house, bingo, instant bingo, lotto, punch cards, and similar games that are legal in a state and are not played against the house. Such gambling may be conducted or may be licensed and regulated by a tribe on tribal lands if it occurs in "a state that permits such gaming for any purpose by any person" and is not prohibited by federal law. Class II gambling is regulated by the tribe and the three-member National Indian Gaming Commission (NIGC), which IGRA created as an independent agency within the Department of the Interior.

- *Class III gambling* consists of all other games: casino gambling, pari-mutuel racing, jai alai, card games played against the house, and electronic facsimiles of games of chance, such as video poker. As with Class II gambling, a tribe may conduct or license these forms of gambling in "a state that permits such gaming for any purpose by any person." Thus, a federal court found, a state that permits charitable organizations to hold occasional "Las Vegas night" fund-raising events has to allow tribes to own full-scale casinos.[11]

    Class III gambling is governed in a unique way: by compacts negotiated between individual states and individual tribes to cover matters such as tribal–state allocations of regulatory authority, the terms of tribal–state criminal justice cooperation, and standards for the operation of gambling facilities, including licensing. Partly because Congress assumed at the time IGRA was enacted that bingo would continue to be the major form of tribal gambling, and partly because Congress wanted the states to be closely consulted in the creation of any casinos, the NIGC's role in Class III gambling was limited to matters such as background investigations of casino investors and managers and approval of casino management contracts.

Congress's expectation about the relative importance that bingo and casino gambling would assume under IGRA could not have been less accurate. As shown in Figure 4.1, by 1998 189 tribes in twenty-four states—that is, 84 percent of the approximately 225 federally recognized tribes in the lower forty-eight states—had Class III casino gambling operations.[12] Of the tribes that did not, some rejected casinos on moral and cultural grounds, such as the Seneca Tribe in New York and the Navajo Nation in Arizona and New Mexico. Other tribes rejected casino gambling because their lands were so distant from population centers that casinos were not economically feasible. Still others would like to open casinos but cannot because they are in states that bar all Class III forms of gambling.

Taken together, the noncasino tribes are few in number but include a majority of the nation's Native American population.[13] Revenues from tribal casinos in one recent year were nearly fifteen times greater than revenues from Class II bingo halls.[14] The largest casino in the western hemisphere, the Foxwoods Resort and Casino in Connecticut, is owned by the Mashantucket Pequot Indians.[15]

In most cases, states and casino-seeking tribes have been able to fulfill their responsibility under IGRA to negotiate mutually acceptable compacts. Each party needed the other: states had concerns about casino-related matters such as traffic congestion, crime, and gambling disorders, and tribes needed state and local cooperation in meeting the increased demand for roads and bridges, water and sewage, fire protection, and electrical service that casino ownership created. In the case of Connecticut and the Pequots, the tribe agreed to give the state 25 percent of its revenues from slot-machine gambling, or a minimum of $100 million per year, in return for the exclusive right to operate slot machines.[16] In other states, tribes successfully employed a strategy

FIGURE 4.1. STATES WITH TRIBAL CASINOS

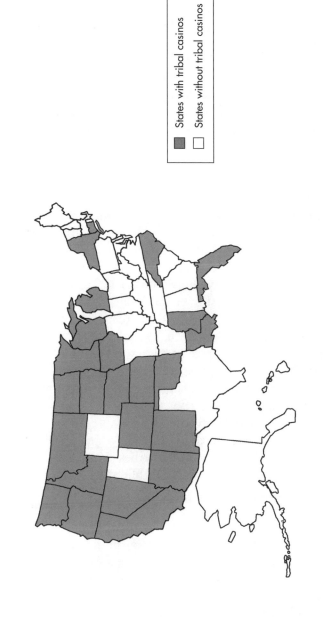

States with tribal casinos

States without tribal casinos

Source: Constructed from data in Abbey Begun, *Gambling: Crime or Recreation?* (Detroit: Gale Group, 2000), p. 28.

that combined "inside lobbying" of the executive branch, the legislature, and the courts with "outside lobbying" (public relations and election campaigns) in their efforts to obtain a compact.[17]

Not all negotiating processes went smoothly, mostly because of resistance from the states; indeed, Connecticut only accepted the inevitability of the Pequot-owned casino after the tribe sued it for not negotiating "in good faith" and won a judgment from a federal court in 1991. The Supreme Court subsequently closed this door to other tribes that were being stonewalled by state governments. In the 1996 case of *Seminole Tribe of Florida* v. *Florida*, the Court voted five to four that the Eleventh Amendment's guarantee to the states of sovereign immunity protects them against lawsuits by American Indian tribes.[18]

Since that case was decided, few states have entered into compacts that had not already done so with at least one tribe. Among those that had not, New Mexico, for example, only abandoned its resistance to tribal casinos after a fiercely fought political campaign by a united coalition of tribes.[19] To be sure, most tribes that wanted casinos had been able to negotiate their compacts before the states realized that they had any choice. But in 1991, in an effort to provide some recourse for tribes still seeking to negotiate compacts with recalcitrant state governments, the Department of the Interior proposed new rule-making procedures that would allow the secretary of the interior to step in. In the face of a lawsuit from Florida and Alabama, however, along with pressure from the National Governors' Association and threatened congressional action to forbid the department from issuing the regulations, the secretary agreed to do nothing until the lawsuit was resolved.

Meanwhile, the state with the largest population by far, California, has decided to grant tribes whose lands are within its borders a monopoly on casino gambling. In 1998, an Indian casino initiative—Proposition 5—was placed on the ballot by tribal organizations. Nevada casino interests, which depend heavily on California gamblers, spent $26 million opposing the initiative, but proponents spent $68 million, making the battle the most expensive initiative campaign in history. Proposition 5 passed by a margin of 63 percent to 37 percent. It was overturned the following year by the California Supreme Court, however, on the grounds that the state constitution had explicitly forbidden casinos in a 1984 amendment that authorized the state to conduct a lottery.

In addition to their efforts on behalf of Proposition 5, California's tribes had poured $7 million into the state's 1998 gubernatorial and legislative campaigns, including more than $650,000 to the winning candidate for governor, Gray Davis. After the election, they spent $2 million lobbying the legislature. In September 1999, a month after the state supreme court ruling, Davis and the legislature agreed to place a constitutional amendment on the March 2000 ballot, Proposition 1A, which would lift the constitution's ban on tribal casinos. Proposition 1A was approved by a margin of 53 percent to 47 percent. Estimates of the number of slot machines that soon will be available in California tribal casinos range from forty thousand to one hundred thousand.[20]

EXPLAINING THE RISE OF TRIBAL GAMBLING

Even more than has been the case with state lotteries and commercial casinos, the rise of tribal gambling has been rapid. Indian casinos are now a familiar part of the national landscape, especially in the West and Midwest. A combination of national political influences and decentralized policymaking accounts for what has happened.

NATIONAL POLITICAL INFLUENCES

National political influences figure heavily in the politics of all forms of legalized gambling, but none more so than in the politics of tribal gambling. The federal government has played an extensive role in shaping public policy in this area, as have interest groups and public opinion.

Federal Government. Every branch of the federal government has helped to hasten the rise of tribal gambling. Several presidents, especially Richard Nixon, Gerald Ford, and Ronald Reagan, promoted economic self-sufficiency on American Indian reservations during the 1970s and 1980s by encouraging tribes to construct revenue-raising bingo halls and, later, casinos. The federal courts opened the floodgates. In 1981, a lower court ruled that a state cannot regulate high-stakes bingo on Native American lands if it permits bingo gambling in any form elsewhere in the state.[21] The Supreme Court's 1987 *Cabazon* ruling explicitly restricted the power of states to prevent gambling facilities from operating on tribal lands, thus ushering in the modern era of tribal casinos.

The legislative branch also has been actively involved in policy-making concerning tribal gambling. In 1988, in an effort to bring some order to state–tribal relations in the aftermath of *Cabazon*, Congress enacted the Indian Gaming Regulatory Act. IGRA acknowledged the political, economic, and sovereign interests of both tribes and states by requiring them to negotiate compacts that would govern the operation of tribal casinos on Indian lands within each state's borders. The act also brought the federal bureaucracy into the process. It created the National Indian Gaming Commission as an independent agency within the Department of the Interior, mostly for the purpose of overseeing the regulation of tribal bingo operations but also to play a limited role in casino gambling. The act charged the secretary of the interior to determine matters such as whether gambling on newly acquired tribal lands was permissible in particular cases.

Interest Groups and Public Opinion. The federal government has not operated in a political vacuum. The civil rights movement of the 1950s and 1960s inspired many groups, including Native Americans, to mobilize for political action. Although the American Indian Movement and the Native American Rights Fund did not organize for the purpose of promoting tribal gambling, they did draw attention to the historic injustices suffered by Indians and helped to create a climate of opinion that was sympathetic to their cause.

One result of the Indian rights movement's efforts is that critics of gambling have tended to pull their punches when it comes to gambling on tribal lands. Robert Goodman of the strongly antigambling United States Gambling Research Institute, for example, is blistering in his criticisms of commercial casinos but notes that "tribes . . . own their casinos. Decisions about casino profits are determined by the tribe, as opposed to a private casino company. . . . As a result, cities and towns rarely see the kinds of benefits from [commercial] casinos which have been found on many Indian reservations."[22] The National Coalition Against Legalized Gambling, an organization that normally gets involved in state campaigns to legalize commercial casinos, played only a small role in California's tribal casino ballot fights in 1998 and 2000.

Public opinion also has become more supportive of tribal gambling. The same antitax, anti-Washington mood that sustained the spread of lotteries in the 1970s and 1980s sustained efforts to make tribes become economically self-sufficient through gambling enterprises. More Americans approve of Indian gambling than of gambling in general because of the economic viability they think it can provide to tribes.[23]

In addition, Americans have become generally more supportive of the justice-based claims of Native Americans, especially when satisfying those claims does not entail new or increased spending by government. Political consultants on both sides of the 1998 California initiative, for example, found that "Indian self-reliance" was the basis for politically persuasive pro-casino arguments. "[T]here's a deep-seated feeling among Americans that Indians have been screwed over the years," said one consultant. "And if [casinos] offered them a chance for some economic self-sufficiency and self-respect, even people who might have reservations about gambling or who weren't gamblers themselves said, 'Look, why not let these folks do this?'" A consultant to the opposition agreed: "Intuitively, people felt it was time to give back the Indians something, because they had been screwed so many times."[24]

Finally, gambling-enriched tribes have become effective players of traditional beltway politics, particularly in the areas of campaign contributions and lobbying. In 1996, tribes gave more than $1.5 million to the Democratic and Republican parties. In 1998 and 2000, in addition to the money tribes spent on their casino campaigns in California, they stepped up their pace of national party contributions. For example, they gave more than $400,000 in soft money to the Democrats and $175,000 to the Republicans during the first four months of 2000 alone.[25] In terms of lobbying, many tribes have secured representation in Washington. The National Congress of American Indians (NCAI), which is headquartered in Washington, represents 250 tribes and works to influence federal decisions that affect tribal operations. As Sue Matson, the president of NCAI, says, "We're [getting] more astute about what Congress listens to, and what Congress listens to is votes and dollars."[26]

DECENTRALIZED POLICYMAKING

Although policymaking concerning tribal gambling is more a matter of national politics than is the case with any other form of legal gambling, the politics of Indian casinos is not entirely centralized. States and tribes are important actors in this area of public policy.

States. The combination of the Supreme Court's *Cabazon* decision in 1987 and Congress's enactment of IGRA in 1988 rendered the role of the states secondary but not peripheral on issues of tribal gambling. States retain constitutional and statutory powers that give them leverage in their dealings with Indian tribes. By declaring illegal all the forms of gambling that IGRA defined as Class II or Class III, for example, a state can close the door to tribal as well as commercial casinos and bingo halls. Conversely, it can legalize commercial casinos and high-stakes bingo gambling, reducing the likelihood that tribal gambling facilities can compete effectively. Short of enacting such extreme measures, a state can choose not to build or improve the roads and bridges that tribal gambling facilities must have to attract customers in large numbers, or it can decline to enforce vigorously the laws that enable casinos to collect delinquent gambling debts.

During the first decade under *Cabazon* and IGRA, few states did more with these powers than use them as negotiating tools. From 1988 to 1997, 147 tribes negotiated casino compacts with the governments of twenty-four states. Unhappy as most of these states were at having large-scale tribal gambling forced on them, they had little choice but to comply: IGRA not only authorized tribes to sue in federal court if a state was not negotiating in good faith, it also placed the evidentiary burden on the state to prove wrong the tribes' charge of bad faith. In the end, many of the state–tribal compacts contained provisions for payments by the tribes to state governments. As noted earlier, the Pequot tribe agreed to turn over a substantial share of its slot machine revenues to the state of Connecticut in return for an exclusivity agreement. Minnesota negotiated a ban with its tribes on all table games except blackjack.

The Court's 1996 ruling in the *Seminole* case freed states from the fear of tribal lawsuits, dramatically enhancing their negotiating position. But in most cases, by the time *Seminole* was decided, the tribes that wanted casinos already had them. In the years since then, most existing tribal casinos have become politically secure: they have a large clientele of gamblers, they employ many workers who are not Native American, and they make substantial campaign contributions to candidates in state and federal elections. It is no coincidence that the greatest opposition to tribal casinos in California initially came not from within the state, but from commercial casino interests in neighboring Nevada.

Tribes. The federal government and, in a much smaller way, the state governments are the crucial policymakers in determining whether American Indian tribes are allowed to operate Class III casinos. But only the tribes themselves can decide if they want to go into the casino business in the first place. It is not enough that some entrepreneurial members of a tribe decide to open a casino. IGRA requires that the tribe as a whole make a collective decision in favor of casino gambling. Most eligible tribes that are close enough to population centers to make casinos economically viable have elected to do so, but some have not.[27]

The line of cleavage that often runs through tribes that are considering gambling divides opponents concerned about tribal culture from supporters whose main goals are economic. Opponents worry that constant dealings with off-reservation casino management companies and other business enterprises will erode their tribes' cultural distinctiveness. They also are concerned that sacred tribal lands will be defiled by highways, parking lots, and golf courses. "We are supposed to be stewards of this land," said a member of the Santa Clara Pueblo tribe in New Mexico, "and we're not very good stewards, allowing all of this stuff to take over."[28] Worried that gambling disorders might spread among tribal members in the same way alcohol addiction has, a Navajo spokesman said, "Many of our people were concerned that those on welfare would run over to a casino with their government checks to win the big payout and end up going hungry."[29]

The Navajo Nation voted against tribal gambling in a 1994 referendum by 55 percent to 45 percent, even though the tribe's economic council had estimated that casinos would generate $30 million per year in revenues and create several thousand jobs. It voted down gambling by a similar margin in 1997. For the great majority of tribes, however, the economic lure of gambling has overwhelmed any cultural concerns. Poor schools, poor health care, low income, high unemployment—these and similar problems, tribal gambling advocates argue, can only be overcome by money, and gambling offers the best opportunity to attract such money to tribal coffers.

THE CONTEMPORARY POLITICS OF TRIBAL GAMBLING

Tribal casinos and bingo halls appeared more rapidly on the landscape of American gambling than state lotteries or commercial casinos. In terms of their consequences, the ink is barely dry on such formative documents as the Supreme Court's *Cabazon* and *Seminole* decisions and the Indian Gaming Regulatory Act. As a result, the contemporary politics of tribal gambling is unusually fluid and unformed. Questions are more readily apparent than answers. Some of these questions are of primary concern to tribes, others are high on the agenda of many states, and still others are being addressed by the federal government.

TRIBES

The United States has seldom allotted land to tribes or allowed tribes to keep their historic lands with the welfare of Native Americans in mind. Through odd quirks of history, some tribes have turned out to be much better situated than others to take advantage of the new opportunities for casino gambling. Specifically, tribes whose lands are near population centers in states whose own laws already allow some form of Class III gambling have been the main beneficiaries of *Cabazon* and IGRA. The Mashantucket Pequots in Connecticut offer the most striking example—they sit squarely in the middle of a multistate market whose population is around twenty-five million. But the Pequots are not unique. Casinos on certain tribal lands in California, Minnesota, Wisconsin, Arizona, and other populous states are similarly well situated.

Most tribal lands, however, are nowhere near population centers. Other such lands are located within states that forbid Class III gambling. The majority of Indian tribes—around 60 percent—are in sparsely populated Alaska, and none of them have tribal casinos. The approximately one hundred gambling facilities that together account for more than 90 percent of all revenues from tribal gambling are owned by less than one-fifth of the tribes. An issue for the new "haves" among Native American tribes, therefore, is what, if anything, to do for the many more tribes that remain "have-nots." This issue has been addressed most directly in California, which as part of its newly drawn state–tribal compacts specifies that a share of tribal casino revenues from slot machines will be distributed among nongambling tribes in the state.

A broader question facing those tribes that are profiting from either casino or bingo gambling is how best to use their revenues. IGRA includes a list of appropriate uses so broad that it serves more as guide than as rule: to fund tribal government operations and programs, to

provide for the general welfare of the tribe and its members, to promote tribal economic development, to support charitable organizations, to help fund the operation of off-reservation local governments,
and, with the approval of the secretary of the interior, to distribute
funds to members of the tribe on a per capita basis.

Some tribal governments that until recently have had few responsibilities and even fewer resources now have many responsibilities
and abundant resources. The issues they confront include: How much
money should be spent on tribal programs, and how much should be
given to individual members of the tribe? How much should be re-
invested in gambling operations, and how much should be invested in
new enterprises that may broaden the tribe's economic base? How
much should be kept by the tribe and how much should be given to
others, including non-Indian charities and less fortunately situated
tribes? Gambling disorders and gambling-related crime are side effects
of casino gambling; how much money should be devoted to reme-
dying such problems, both on the reservation and in surrounding
communities? A complicating aspect of all these issues is the desire of
most tribes to retain their cultural distinctiveness even as they become
big businesses in the mainstream economy and major players in the
political arena.

STATES

Most tribal governments in the lower forty-eight states have been
enthusiastic participants in the recent rise of American Indian gambling. The federal government, relieved that many of these tribes have
developed a plausible strategy for economic self-sufficiency that does
not involve new federal spending, has been broadly supportive of
their efforts.

The states have been alone among the sovereign levels of government in their widespread dislike, even resentment, of tribal gambling. Their attitude is understandable. Most of the states that now
have tribal casinos and high-stakes bingo halls operating within their
borders have consistently rejected commercial casinos and high-stakes
bingo gambling. As a matter of public policy, they simply have not
wanted these forms of gambling in their states.

States also have resented the assumption embedded in IGRA that
bad faith on their part is the likely explanation when state–tribal negotiations concerning Class III gambling do not produce a compact. As

one state attorney general told the National Gambling Impact Study Commission, "any legitimate difference of opinion results in somebody hoist[ing] the bad faith flag, and it only goes against one party, the state."[30] In addition, states have felt aggrieved that most of the problems generated by tribal gambling—especially traffic congestion, gambling-related crime, and gambling disorders—fall on them even though they cannot tax the incomes of tribal casinos or even tribal members who work for the casinos to cover the costs of addressing these problems.

The attitudes of many state governments have softened somewhat in recent years. Tribal gambling operations are major employers, and the great majority of their employees are not Native Americans. When these employees leave the reservation at the end of the working day, they take their wages and salaries into the state's economy and pay taxes into the state treasury. In addition, most state–tribal compacts include some provision for contributions by the tribe to the state. The Pequot tribe is the largest single contributor to the Connecticut state treasury.

The major contemporary question facing the states is whether to embrace tribal gambling enterprises in the same way that they embrace other major employers, or continue to hold them at arm's length. This is a public policy question, but it may receive a purely political answer. Increasingly, tribes are channeling campaign contributions into state elections and hiring lobbyists in state capitals. They also are mobilizing the votes of their nontribal employees. In many ways, therefore, the contemporary state politics of tribal casinos verges on becoming politics as usual.

FEDERAL GOVERNMENT

Two major issues concerning tribal gambling currently preoccupy federal policymakers. One is what to do when tribes seek to acquire land for new gambling facilities. The other, which forced its way onto the federal agenda with the Supreme Court's 1996 *Seminole* ruling, involves situations in which states and tribes are unable to negotiate compacts for Class III gambling.

New Land for Gambling. IGRA's general rule is that tribal gambling can occur only on lands that tribes possessed before the law was enacted in 1988. It allows certain exceptions, however. Most of these exceptions are for landless tribes that acquire land to which they have historic or other legitimate claims. But the exception that has loomed largest and proved most controversial involves tribes that purchase off-reservation land for the purpose of opening a gambling facility. Such efforts require the approval of both the secretary of the interior and the governor of the affected state.

Several tribes have tried to purchase new land for gambling, usually as a strategy to gain access to population centers distant from their reservations. In some cases, local governments in declining areas, often encouraged by gambling interests, even have tried to entice tribes to acquire nearby land in hopes of fostering economic development. Of the ten applications for off-reservation land purchases that tribes filed with the Department of the Interior between 1988 and 1999, only two were approved. One of the rejected applications reveals just how controversial such efforts can be. In 1997, when Secretary Bruce Babbitt rejected an application by three Chippewa tribes to purchase a Wisconsin dog track located between Milwaukee and Chicago and convert it to a casino, he was charged with having succumbed to political pressure from five other tribes that opposed the application and that together donated around $300,000 to the Democratic Party. After a nineteen-month investigation, an independent counsel appointed to look into the matter exonerated Babbitt.[31] But the political explosiveness of the process of seeking exceptions remains undiminished, especially when tribes already operating gambling facilities perceive a threat from other tribes seeking to enter their markets.

Impasses in Compact Negotiations. Realizing that not all negotiations end in agreement, Congress provided in IGRA that if a state and a tribe could not negotiate a compact for Class III tribal gambling, the tribe could seek to persuade a federal court to impose a compact. In May 1996, less than two months after the Supreme Court struck down this provision in the *Seminole* case, the Bureau of Indian Affairs published a proposed rule in the *Federal Register* that would empower the secretary of the interior to impose a Class III compact if he or she determined that the state was not negotiating in good faith. Congress responded by passing a law that temporarily forbade the secretary to approve such a compact without the state's permission. When the law expired in early 1999 and the proposed final rule was published, Florida and Alabama filed suit in federal court. Facing further congressional action, Babbitt promised not to implement the rule until the lawsuit ran its course.

Not only is the question of state–tribal compacts unresolved, so is the status of the casinos that some tribes are operating outside of any negotiated compact. (Tribes call them "uncompacted" casinos, states call them "illegal.") Currently, more than a quarter of all tribal casinos are operating without compacts.[32] Because states lack the constitutional authority to act against these tribes, they must rely on the federal government, specifically the Department of Justice, to do so.[33] But the Justice Department has not been eager to get involved in what seem to many to be political disputes.

POLICY RECOMMENDATIONS

On balance, we regard tribal gambling as a useful strategy to attain a measure of self-sufficiency for a group of Americans that historically has been downtrodden. Nonetheless, governments at the state and federal level have distinct issues to address. So, in our view, do tribal governments, but to them our recommendations are offered with particular diffidence, in full awareness that the "domestic" policy of American Indian tribes is more a matter of tribal than of general concern.

TRIBES

Most of our recommendations concern tribes that are operating successful gambling facilities. These recommendations have two closely interwoven purposes. One is to help the tribes become self-sufficient. The other is to encourage them to accept certain responsibilities along with their success.

We recommend first that tribes invest a substantial amount, perhaps the majority, of their profits from casinos and bingo halls in efforts to diversify their economic enterprises. Although gambling revenues may seem bottomless to highly successful tribes such as the Pequots in Connecticut, they are anything but secure. If neighboring New York, Massachusetts, or Rhode Island were to legalize casino gambling, the market advantage currently enjoyed by the Foxwoods casino would vanish. Moreover, one need only note the experience of the horse racing industry to see how quickly fortunes based in gambling ventures can plummet.

By using some of the proceeds from gambling as seed money to enter or expand other industries, as the Ojibwe tribe in Minnesota has done with the fishing industry and the Oneida Nation in New York has done with organic farming,[34] Indian tribes with substantial populations can take long strides toward sustainable economic independence. Other possibilities for economic development, which are especially suitable when natural resources on the reservation are scarce or the reservation is far from any large population center, include light manufacturing and the production and marketing of Native American art. Small tribes that find it impractical to operate a diversity of businesses can at least diversify their investments.

Expanding the range of economic enterprises may not be enough to ensure tribal self-sufficiency. We recommend that, whenever feasible, the management of Indian gambling facilities be handled by members of the tribe. Tribes should treat management contracts with private gambling companies as short-term expedients designed primarily to help them learn the business themselves. In keeping with the goal of self-sufficiency, the expertise employees derive by becoming experienced at casino and resort management, business administration, and government–business relations ought to remain within the tribe as much as possible.

Some of the larger Native American tribes in California that have had gambling operations on their reservations since the 1980s serve as good examples of economic self-sufficiency. These tribes' leaders and workers shed their reliance on outside management. They also became savvy enough at building political capital through campaign contributions and public relations efforts to bring about the passage of tribal casino propositions in 1998 and 2000.[35]

In addition to improving the business and political skills of their members, we urge tribes that offer casino and bingo gambling to work with state governments to address gambling disorders on and near tribal lands. Although there is some evidence that Native Americans are more prone to gambling disorders than whites,[36] the studies that have produced this evidence are few and, in most cases, are based on very small samples. No one doubts, however, that gambling disorders on reservations have grown since tribes got into the gambling business. We recommend that tribes both set aside a portion of their gambling revenues to treat tribal members and, through amendments to state–tribal compacts, channel additional revenues to states to treat other customers of theirs who experience gambling disorders.

As the paucity of studies on gambling disorders among American Indians illustrates, ample and reliable information, which is crucial to sound policymaking concerning tribal gambling, is in short supply. Regrettably, many tribes, and even the National Indian Gaming Commission, failed to provide the National Gambling Impact Study Commission with data about tribes' financial holdings, unemployment rates, changes in infrastructure, and contributions to surrounding communities.[37] In our view, the claim by tribes that such information is "proprietary," although rooted in longstanding concerns about tribal dignity and sovereignty,[38] is insufficiently persuasive. After all, the federal government has permitted and even condoned tribal gambling as a means of helping Native Americans to become self-sufficient. The NIGC, as a federal agency, stands on even weaker ground when it withholds data. Considering the importance of the decisions about gambling that all levels of government are making, the more information that is available to the public and to policymakers, the better.

STATES

The primary reason that states need all the information they can get regarding tribal gambling is that they have a great deal at stake when casinos and high-stakes bingo halls begin to operate within their borders. Not only are state governments called on to provide roads and bridges so that customers can travel to and from tribal gambling facilities, they also are burdened in less direct ways, such as providing welfare, housing, treatment, and law enforcement to their citizens who have developed gambling disorders. We especially sympathize with the concerns of states that have had to accept tribal casinos within their borders even though their own laws exclude commercial casinos.

Nevertheless, states must act in good faith so that tribes can exercise their sovereign rights and advance toward self-sufficiency. We recommend to states that already permit nontribal Class III gambling that they fulfill the charge in IGRA to negotiate compacts with any remaining interested tribes that are located within their borders. States that refuse to do so violate the letter of IGRA and the intent of the Indian Self-Determination and Education Assistance Act of 1975, which codified the federal policy of tribal self-sufficiency. States that negotiate in good faith have every reason to expect tribes to respond in kind.

When conducting these negotiations, a state's concern should extend not just to tribes seeking a compact but also to other tribes located within its borders that for reasons of culture, morality, or economic feasibility have not sought to offer gambling. In some ways, these tribes are worse off in the era of tribal gambling than in the past because of the widespread misperception that every problem that besets Native Americans has been solved by gambling. Therefore, states should seek to amend compacts either to compel tribes that offer gambling to share some of their revenues with tribes that do not, or, alternatively, to offer incentives, perhaps in the form of reduced payments to the state, to tribes that share their wealth with other tribes.

A final word to the states: neither *Cabazon* nor IGRA forces any state to allow forms of gambling that it does not wish to allow. States have the right to bar unwanted types of gambling from tribal and nontribal lands by refusing to legalize any form of gambling, as Tennessee, Utah, and Hawaii have done.

FEDERAL GOVERNMENT

We regret that, in writing IGRA, Congress defined Class III gambling as expansively as it did. In essence, the statutory language describing the coverage of Class III gambling ("a state that permits such gaming for any purpose by any person") forces a state that has rejected commercial casino gambling to allow tribes to operate casinos if the state also allows, for example, charitable organizations to hold occasional "Las Vegas Nights" as fund-raisers. At the time IGRA was enacted, Congress should have distinguished more carefully among the variety of state-level policies regarding gambling.

That said, we acknowledge that changing the law now would have very little effect on the state–tribal politics of gambling. In the great majority of eligible cases, states and tribes have already negotiated compacts. Casinos are up and running. To close them down at this point would be a substantial hardship for tribes that have acted in good faith.

Similarly, in the aftermath of the 1996 *Seminole* decision protecting states against tribal lawsuits, those few tribes that have been denied authority to operate casinos because of state recalcitrance have experienced a hardship. Therefore, we urge federal officials to execute the intent of IGRA insofar as it is meant to give tribes some recourse when states will not negotiate in good faith. Specifically, we recommend that procedures that allow the secretary of the interior to impose a compact in extreme instances be approved and implemented.

We also recommend that the secretary review with skepticism any application by a tribe to acquire off-reservation land for gambling operations.[39] Such applications may represent efforts by local governments and gambling interests to use tribes in order to get casinos in states where commercial casinos are illegal. Officials in a city such as Beaumont, Texas (a state in which charitable bingo, charitable games, and lottery wagering are legal but tribal and commercial casinos are not), may try to sell land to a tribe at a nominal cost in the hope of attracting jobs and capital investment. Whether this occurs in Texas or any other state, we think it unseemly because the citizens of the state would end up with casinos in their midst without having had any voice in such a major policy change. In essence, those who serve as secretary of the interior have it within their power to keep this Pandora's box closed, and we recommend that they do so.

Our final recommendation to the federal government is meant to further everyone's understanding of tribal gambling. Congress should see to it that tribes submit relevant information to appropriate federal agencies about the effects their gambling activities have on local environments, along with other useful information, such as the amount of revenue that tribes spend on tribal government operations and programs, economic development, and the other purposes listed in IGRA. Specifically, Congress should make taxpayer-funded assistance to the tribes contingent on their doing so, just as federal highway funding is contingent on states enforcing a twenty-one-year-old drinking age. As with other forms of gambling, the more that is known about tribal gambling and its consequences, the better informed the national climate of opinion will be.

5

THE FEDERAL ROLE

State and local governments often feel hamstrung by the federal government. Conditions of aid—the strings attached to federal grant programs—typically deny funds from the national treasury to states and localities unless they configure their policies to conform with federal standards. Federal mandates are sticks without carrots; they simply require state and local governments to comply with policies established in Washington. In addition, federal criminal law increasingly extends into areas that traditionally have been left to the states.

The federal government has played a decidedly secondary role with regard to gambling, however. Washington was a bystander as lotteries spread from one state in 1964 to thirty-eight states and the District of Columbia by 2000. Even the quasi-national Powerball and Big Game lotteries arose from state initiatives. Nearly all of the policies that govern commercial casinos, pari-mutuel betting, and charitable gambling also have been made at the state level.

Necessarily, the federal government has been a much more influential participant in policymaking toward tribal casinos, although most of its efforts have been aimed at fostering cooperation between state and tribal governments. Threats of federal action in other areas of gambling policy, especially policy concerning commercial casinos, have been rare but politically significant. News that the Clinton administration was seriously considering a gambling tax to help fund its welfare reform program was all that it took to mobilize the commercial casino industry to establish the American Gaming Association in 1994. The industry was equally alarmed when Congress considered the 1996 bill sponsored by Democratic senator Paul Simon of Illinois and Republican representative Frank Wolf of Virginia to create the National Gambling Impact Study Commission (NGISC). Since the mid-1990s, casino companies, associations, and executives have been major contributors to the Republican and Democratic parties. A single tribe, the Mashantucket Pequots of Connecticut, donated around $1 million to the Democratic Party during the 1990s.[1]

Other developments are likely to spark increasing federal interest in gambling policy. Three of these developments are discussed in this chapter. First, the rise and rapid spread of the Internet has sparked the creation of many gambling websites. Because nearly all of these sites operate outside the boundaries of any single state—indeed, most of them are based in foreign countries—the federal government necessarily has become the primary arena of politics and policy. Second, the interstate and often Internet-based character of sports betting also necessitates a federal role. Third, the work of the NGISC has placed the federal government squarely at the center of the nation's research effort concerning gambling. The commission's leading finding was that gambling's rapid rise on the American scene has been unaccompanied by any broad or deep understanding of its social and economic consequences. "Legalized gambling on a wide scale is a new phenomenon in modern America," the NGISC's final report noted, "and much of the relevant research is in its infancy."[2] In other matters of national concern, it has been the federal government that traditionally has stimulated the research necessary to bridge the chasm between scientific understanding and public policy.

We conclude our discussion of the federal role in gambling policy by offering a set of recommendations. Some of these recommendations concern Internet gambling, others concern sports betting, and still others have to do with the federal government's role in research.

INTERNET GAMBLING

The Internet is the most rapidly spreading medium in history. It took radio thirty-eight years to reach fifty million users. Television spread more quickly, attaining the fifty million mark in thirteen years. The Internet reached its fifty millionth user just five years after it became readily available. As with radio and television, the United States led the way. Estimates vary, but at least half of the more than two hundred million Internet users in the world today are Americans.[3]

The effects of the Internet on gambling have been considerable. *Wired* magazine declared that "Cyberspace is gambling's next frontier" in 1995, the same year that the first gambling website opened.[4] By 1999, more than 500 gambling sites were available online: one study listed 250 online casinos, 64 lotteries, 20 bingo games, and 139 sports books.[5] An analyst for Christiansen/Cummings Associates conservatively calculated that Internet gambling revenues doubled from $300 million in 1997 to $651 million in 1998, then redoubled to $1.2 billion in 1999.[6] An estimated fifteen million Americans gambled on the Internet in 1998, more than twice the seven million who were thought to have done so the previous year. Other industry analysts offer still higher estimates of Internet usage by gamblers.[7]

One of the reasons that the data on Internet gambling are so imprecise is that its legal status in the United States is murky. In this section we chronicle the rapid rise of Internet gambling, then assess the contemporary politics that surround it, especially at the federal level.

THE RISE OF INTERNET GAMBLING

The rapid rise of Internet gambling has required more than just the spread of Internet access to many millions of American homes, offices, dorm rooms and libraries. It also has entailed a wide availability of gambling websites, along with secure means for wagers to be transmitted from bettors to casinos and for winnings to be sent from casinos to bettors.

Foreign governments have provided a legal setting for gambling websites to register and operate in Australia, a host of Caribbean nations, and several countries in Europe. These websites can be accessed by American Internet users as easily as websites whose servers are housed next door. With some exceptions, banks and credit card companies have provided secure means for transferring wagers and winnings between bettors and offshore Internet casinos.

A handful of states have passed laws to make gambling on the Internet illegal, and Florida has persuaded Western Union not to send money transfers from that state to forty offshore sports books. But the states themselves recognize the limits of their enforceable authority. In a move that was unusual in its plea for federal rather than state action, the National Association of Attorneys General recently called on the federal government to expand its authority over Internet gambling.

The federal government has not been unresponsive to the states' concerns. Invoking the Wire Communications Act of 1961, for example, the Department of Justice has prosecuted American citizens who own gambling websites, even though the sites were legally registered in foreign countries. "You can't hide on line and you can't hide offshore," former Attorney General Janet Reno recently proclaimed. The Justice Department argues that the wire act extends to Internet gambling and has won at least one conviction in federal district court on that basis.[8]

Many others believe that the wire act's usefulness has been strained severely by the Internet. One reason is that the act, which bars the use of wire communications to place bets on "sporting events or contests," was passed for the purpose of preventing telephones and telegraphs from being employed to wager on horse races and athletic competitions. Its applicability to online lotteries and casino games, much less to an Internet industry that is moving from a reliance on telephone wires to cellular, fiberoptic, and satellite technologies, is tenuous.[9] Still worse, even a broad interpretation of the act leaves its enforceability against online wagering in jeopardy. Americans who wish to gamble in online casinos that are registered in other countries need only dial one of many overseas Internet Service Providers (ISPs) in order to cover their digital tracks before connecting with a gambling website.[10]

Meanwhile, Internet gambling by Americans continues to expand—from the estimated $1.2 billion that was wagered in 1999 to a projected $2 billion in 2000 and $3 billion or more in 2002.[11] Several reasons account for this expansion. More Americans are becoming wired and, as they do so, are spending more time on the Internet. Technological advances continue to make it faster and easier to download from gambling websites the software needed to play games and place bets, and the speed of the games (which has been slow) is increasing. With experience, Internet users are becoming more confident in general about the safety and security of online financial transactions. Underlying these Internet-related developments is the appetite of Americans who lack ready access to traditional "bricks-and-mortar" casinos to play casino games.

CONTEMPORARY POLITICS

Proposals to legalize Internet gambling thus far have won little support among voters, political parties, interest groups, or political leaders at either the state or federal level. A 1999 Gallup poll found that "legalized gambling or betting using the Internet" was approved by 20 percent and disapproved by 75 percent of voters, by far the largest margin of public opposition to any form of gambling.[12] The only group that has lobbied in favor of Internet gambling in recent legislative controversies has been the Interactive Gaming Council, an association of web-based casinos and sports books that is located in Vancouver, Canada. Thus, unlike lotteries and casinos, the contemporary politics of Internet gambling has been less a matter of deciding whether it is a good thing or a bad thing than of deciding what the problems are and whether appropriate remedies are available to policymakers who wish to address these problems.

Problems. The most widely discussed problems with Internet gambling fall into three categories: gambling disorders, especially among young people; crime; and burdens on government.

Gambling disorders have many causes and can occur in virtually any environment, but the temptation that Internet gambling offers to those who are prone to gamble excessively is unique. For the large and rapidly increasing number of Americans who have online access through their personal computers, gambling websites are a twenty-four-hour-a-day, seven-day-a-week presence in their homes. Young people, most of whom have grown up with the Internet, may be especially susceptible to the lures of web-based gambling. Playing online games of one sort or another is nothing new to them, and they are accustomed to sending money over the Internet with their own or their parents' credit cards. Gambling websites typically accept the word of bettors who claim to be of legal age. Both as a potentially addictive form of gambling in its own right and as a gateway to other dangerous forms, Internet gambling contributes to gambling disorders.

Internet gambling also may foster crime in a distinctive and especially problematic way. Until recently, casinos provided a setting in which cash-rich criminal organizations could "launder" money: their minions simply bought chips with illegally obtained cash, played a little, then cashed in the chips for untainted currency. Congress closed this door in the mid-1980s by requiring casinos to report every transaction larger than $10,000 to the federal government. Internet casinos, however, are not as easily regulated because they are registered in foreign countries. Their doors thus stand wide open to money laundering.

A final problem associated with Internet gambling involves its effect on government. Unlike legal forms of gambling, offshore-based gambling websites pay no taxes to state governments. Nor do they generate the jobs and capital investment that casinos and racetracks do. Yet states are left to deal with the problems some of their citizens develop as a result of excessive gambling, including crime and bankruptcy. In addition, state governments and the federal government only receive income taxes from successful Internet gamblers who voluntarily report their winnings, a considerably smaller number than those whose winnings are reported directly to governments by commercial and tribal casinos, lottery agencies, and racetracks.

Proposed Remedies. The will to prevent Internet gambling has been widespread in Washington. Strong uncertainties remain about the way. Much of Congress's attention in recent years has been devoted to the proposed Internet Gambling Prohibition Act. The bill first was introduced by Republican senator Jon Kyl of Arizona in 1997, a year in which the number of gambling websites was still around sixty. In its current form, the Kyl bill would extend the coverage of the 1961 Wire Communications Act to include Internet-related technologies such as fiberoptic cable and microwave transmission. (An undersea fiberoptic cable already links Antigua, where Internet gambling is legal, to the United States.) The bill offers an exemption to the pari-mutuel industry that allows bets on races to be placed on the Internet through "closed-door subscriber-based systems" of the kind described in Chapter 3. It also allows the states to sell lottery tickets over the Internet.

The Kyl bill, important in its own right, is even more significant as a window into the complex politics of Internet gambling. The bill has passed the Senate overwhelmingly on three occasions, twice during the 105th Congress and once in 1999. Strong support has been provided by an unusual political coalition. A broad spectrum of Christian groups favors the bill, ranging from the liberal National Council of Churches, which regards gambling as a threat to the poor, to the conservative Southern Baptist Convention and Focus on the Family, which are concerned primarily with issues of morality. These groups are joined by the American Gaming Association, which represents established and closely regulated bricks-and-mortar casinos, and by amateur and professional sports organizations such as the National Football League (NFL), Major League Baseball (MLB), and the National Collegiate Athletic

Association (NCAA), which worry about the effects of Internet-based sports betting on the integrity of their games.

The House version of the Kyl bill, sponsored by Republican representative Bob Goodlatte of Virginia, has sparked an even more unusual set of political alliances. It differs from the Senate version in not exempting state lotteries from its coverage, a modification that has roused the opposition of some state governors but has won the support of the National Association of Convenience Stores, whose members do not want to lose lottery ticket sales to the Internet.

Goodlatte's version came before the full House in July 2000 under a procedure that limited debate and barred amendments from the floor but also required a two-thirds majority for passage. A furious round of lobbying ensued. The Vancouver-based Interactive Gaming Council lobbied in opposition to the bill. House members from districts with large high-tech industries were pressured not to restrict the Internet in any way. The Traditional Values Coalition broke ranks with other Christian organizations to oppose the bill because of the protection it offered to the horse racing industry. The coalition was joined in this objection by the Clinton administration, which interpreted the wire act as already applying to Internet gambling and argued that the exemption for pari-mutuel betting would "expand gambling."[13] Although the vote was 245 to 159 in favor of the bill, it fell twenty-five votes short of the required two-thirds. Democrats provided 70 percent of the opposition votes.

Not all of the doubts about the Kyl bill have come from its opponents. Even some who share the bill's goals worry about its effectiveness in achieving those goals. For example, the NGISC declined to endorse the bill because the commissioners felt that it had been watered down through numerous amendments and exemptions. In addition, federal law by its nature does not extend to the offshore-based websites at which most Internet gambling takes place. "Congress is waving a butterfly net at the wind," attorneys Richard Raysman and Peter Brown have argued.[14]

SPORTS BETTING

Estimates of how much is bet each year on professional and collegiate sporting events vary wildly, from as low as $85 billion to as high as $400 billion. The reason for this indeterminacy is that the vast majority of sports betting that occurs in the United States is illegal and thus goes unreported to the Internal Revenue Service, the Securities and Exchange Commission, or any other federal or state entity. Almost all of the legal betting on sports occurs in the sports betting parlors (called "sports books") of Nevada casinos. But the $2.4 billion in wagers on sports that these sports books took in during 1997 constituted no more than 3 percent—and perhaps as little as 1 percent—of the estimated amount that Americans bet on sports that year.[15]

THE RISE OF SPORTS BETTING

Unlike Internet gambling, sports betting has deep historical roots. In the early twentieth century, Arnold Rothstein, a New York crime figure, developed the "layoff" system that allows bookmakers to accept large bets with the confidence that they can spread the risk by distributing some of these bets among their fellow bookmakers around the country.[16] Organized crime has been deeply involved in sports betting ever since.

Nevada first authorized casinos to offer sports betting in 1931, when the state legalized casino gambling. Although never the most profitable part of their operations, casinos use sports books to draw customers in the hope that they also will gamble on slots or table games that yield a higher return to the house.

The bad effects of sports betting also have a history. Rothstein himself bribed players on the Chicago White Sox to lose the 1919 World Series in the notorious "Black Sox Scandal." Between 1947 and 1950, thirty-two players at seven colleges and universities were implicated in fixing games or shaving points.[17] In 1951, rigged college games became a national scandal when seven players on the championship City College of New York basketball team confessed to shaving points.

Responding to the City College scandal, Congress voted in 1951 to impose a 10 percent excise tax on winnings from sports gambling, whether legal or illegal. The 1961 Wire Communications Act, which bans the use of telegraph and telephones to place bets on sporting events, was designed explicitly to undermine illegal sports betting and, more generally, to force organized crime out of gambling. In the mid-1970s, however, Congress was persuaded that the excise tax was driving customers from legal sports betting to illegal sports betting. It reduced the tax on winnings to 2 percent in 1974 and to 0.25 percent in 1983.

Until the 1990s, the federal government did nothing to prevent states from legalizing sports betting. California, New York, Illinois, and New Jersey were among the states that considered doing so in the late 1980s. Finally, sports industry leaders such as the NFL, MLB, and the National Basketball Association (NBA) pressured Congress to forbid state-sanctioned and state-sponsored sports betting. These organizations worried about the actual and perceived integrity of their games, fearing that every missed shot, fumble, and called third strike would become suspect. Even one points-shaving scandal every few years, for example, could undermine basketball's widespread popularity. "Gambling and sports do not mix," said Red Auerbach, president of the Boston Celtics, while testifying for the NBA in a 1992 House Judiciary subcommittee hearing.[18]

On the other side of the issue, state governments and the North American Association of State and Provincial Lotteries (NASPL) lobbied Congress to continue to allow states to legalize sports betting. States never like to see a potential source of revenue taken off the table, and NASPL regarded lottery games based on sporting contests as a way to increase lottery ticket sales. For example, after the Oregon lottery tied one of its games to the outcome of NFL football games, its revenues increased substantially.

In the end, the sports industry got its way. On October 28, 1992, the Professional and Amateur Sports Protection Act took effect. The act forbids betting on professional and amateur sports, exempting only Oregon, Nevada, Montana, and Delaware, which had already legalized sports betting. (Montana and Delaware never implemented their laws.) Pari-mutuel betting on horse and dog racing and on jai alai was exempted in every state.

Nevada and its 142 sports books are the source of the famous "point spreads" or "Las Vegas line,"[19] published in newspapers around the country. Although point spreads technically pertain only to legal sports betting in Nevada, bookies everywhere in the country use them in their own illegal betting operations. Critics of gambling claim that the line contributes less to the popularity of sports than to the popularity of sports betting.

CONTEMPORARY POLITICS

A number of national forces, including Americans' demand for gambling, their vast interest in sporting events, and the widespread publication of point spreads, make illegal sports betting rampant today. That most sports betting is illegal, however, is not the only problem that it poses.

Problems. Perhaps the primary problem with sports betting is that many young people appear to enter into gambling disorders through the gateway of sports betting.[20] In a poll taken by Gallup in May 1999, 27 percent of teenagers reported that they had bet on a professional sporting event in the past year. Only 13 percent of adults reported that they had done so. Moreover, 18 percent of teenagers reported that they had bet on a college sporting event in the past year, double the 9 percent of adults who reported having placed such a bet.[21] A 1997 Harvard study found that the rate of disordered gambling among college students was 4.7 percent, roughly three times the 1.6 percent rate among adults.[22] Together, these data indicate that gambling—particularly sports gambling—is a problem that plagues many young people.

A vast market of young people with disposable income and an interest—sometimes an overwhelming interest—in sporting events exists in collegiate settings. Bookies are quick to enter such a market. For example, one student at the University of Florida admitted to taking illegal bets on sporting events for two years; even more troubling, he claimed that at least ten other Florida students were doing the same thing. At times, sports gambling can lead to violence or the threat of violence. Michael Beckerman, another University of Florida student, was arrested for hiring a man to collect a gambling debt from a fellow student by "any means necessary—including breaking fingers and toes." Unfortunately, it usually takes arrests such as this one, rather than the mere evidence that illegal gambling is widespread on campus, to force college administrators into action.[23]

A second problem with sports betting is that fair athletic contests may be corrupted or undermined by gambling dollars. In the 1990s alone, sports betting scandals were uncovered at more than ten schools, including Arizona State University, Boston College, the University of Maryland, Northwestern University, Bryant College, and Columbia University. The NCAA is aware of what is occurring. "The influence of sports gambling is far reaching . . . and student bookies are present at every institution," says Bill Saum, the NCAA's antigambling staff member.[24]

The NCAA, the NFL, and all other major sporting organizations regard as absolutely essential the confidence fans have in the integrity and fairness of their games. Otherwise, as then–New Jersey senator Bill Bradley warned during the floor debate on the 1992 Professional and Amateur Sports Protection Act, sports "would become the gambler's game and not the fan's game. And athletes would become roulette chips."[25] Another argument against sports betting is that if contests are fixed ahead of time, the viewer is only witnessing a scripted event, not unlike a previously taped sitcom or professional wrestling show.

Finally, the illegal nature of sports betting creates opportunities for organized crime, which during the last thirty years has been largely rooted out of the corporation-dominated casino industry. In 1998, for example, a Columbia alumnus and a law student at New York University were arrested for taking bets on sporting events from other students. The wagers were telephoned to a gambling ring operated by an organized crime figure who previously had been convicted in federal court for racketeering and the murder of a police detective.[26] More generally, as NCAA executive director Cedric Dempsey testified to the National Gambling Impact Study Commission, "We are seeing an increase in the involvement of organized crime in sports wagering."[27]

Proposed Remedies. With the exception of the Professional and Amateur Sports Protection Act of 1992, efforts to end illegal sports betting have been few. Until very recently, most of these efforts have come from nongovernmental entities, especially the professional and amateur sports organizations.

The NFL, MLB, and the NBA have established strict penalties for those who gamble on sports. Any player or coach who bets on his own sport may be dismissed immediately. Baseball's continuing refusal to admit Pete Rose to the Baseball Hall of Fame indicates how strictly this policy is enforced. The NCAA forbids student athletes and athletic department staff members from betting on college or professional sports. Those who violate this rule can be expelled or dismissed and fined.[28] The NCAA also tries to investigate any violations that it uncovers or that are brought to its attention.[29]

In 2000, the NCAA supported the Amateur Sports Integrity Act, a bill sponsored in the Senate by Republican John McCain and in the House by Republican Lindsey Graham and Democrat Tim Roemer. The bill would close the "Las Vegas loophole" in the 1992 Professional and Amateur Sports Protection Act that allows gambling in Nevada on college sports. It pits the Nevada casino industry against the NCAA. Both of these organizations are powerful lobbying forces in Washington, but, in the 1999–2000 election cycle, Nevada-based casino corporations strengthened their political position by donating $2.35 million of soft money to the Republican Party and $1.55 million to the Democratic Party, more than double the amount they had donated in the previous presidential election cycle.[30]

Even if the Amateur Sports Integrity Act were to pass, a newspaper industry group, the Newspaper Association of America (NAA), has said that its members would continue to publish the point spreads of upcoming college games. NAA president John F. Sturm claimed that the "point spreads appear to be useful, if not valuable, to newspaper readers who have no intention of betting on games."[31]

Two less-noticed sports betting bills also have been introduced in the House. The Illegal Sports Betting Enforcement Act of 2000 would create a federal task force within the Department of Justice to study and enforce federal laws regarding illegal sports betting. The Combating Illegal College and University Gambling Act would create a panel of federal officials and charge it to conduct a study of college sports gambling, to advise the NCAA about how to enforce laws, and to examine the effectiveness of the steps taken by colleges and universities to reduce the problem.

RESEARCH

Historically, national study commissions have been a leading consumer and sponsor of scholarly research on issues of public policy. The NGISC was no exception. It not only canvassed the existing literature on gambling but also devoted nearly half of its $5 million budget to initiating new research on topics such as gambling behavior, the treatment of gambling disorders, and the operations of state lotteries. Yet, "one of our most important conclusions," wrote commission chair Kay C. James in the final report, "is that far more data is needed in virtually every area."[32] The commission unanimously concluded that "the available information on the economic and social impact [of gambling] is spotty at best and usually inadequate for an informed discussion let alone decision."[33] Indeed, the commission's major recommendation—namely, for "a pause in the extension of gambling"[34]—was rooted in its alarm at the haste with which state and local governments had been legalizing new forms of gambling in the absence of an informed understanding of what the likely consequences would be.

The commission was thwarted to some extent in its efforts to gather relevant information. Responding to pressure from the American Gaming Association, the Senate stripped from the House-passed bill to create the commission a provision that would have allowed it to subpoena individuals to testify at its hearings. After the commission had begun its work, most American Indian tribes and the National Indian Gaming Commission rebuffed requests for information from the commission,[35] a practice that, if continued, will hamper other research efforts in the future.

A more fundamental problem, however, is the dearth of existing scholarly research on gambling. To be sure, historians have studied gambling extensively, drawing attention to the ways that political sentiment and governmental response have varied over the years.[36] Scholars in other disciplines also have contributed to the literature on gambling. Psychologists and sociologists have been interested in the causes and treatment of gambling disorders. Economists have studied the costs and benefits of gambling for local economies and state treasuries.

Unfortunately, the efforts thus far have been insufficient. The National Research Council's commission-sponsored review of the literature on gambling disorders, for example, lamented "past studies that utilized 'methods so inadequate as to invalidate their conclusions,' the absence of 'systematic data,' the substitution of 'assumptions for the missing data,' the lack of testing of assumptions, 'haphazard' applications of estimations in one study by another, the lack of clear identification of the costs and benefits to be studied, and many other problems."[37] As for the economic research on gambling, much of it has been sponsored by either opponents of gambling or proponents of new gambling enterprises.[38] Even nonpartisan economic research has led to dramatically different conclusions.

The absence of a well-developed body of research on gambling is attributable in part to the long-established priorities of federal and state research agencies, in which the topic of gambling often falls between the cracks. One of the results of this neglect is an impoverished debate on gambling's causes and consequences. For every research-based claim about the virtues of gambling, there seems to be an equal and opposite research-based counterclaim. For example, after economist Earl L. Grinols testified to Congress that compulsive gamblers account for the bulk of casino revenues, the director of the Institute for the Study of Gambling, William L. Eadington, dismissed his data as "back-of-envelope" calculations.[39]

To say that nothing can be learned from the existing body of research on gambling would be unfair. Some especially good work has been done on gambling disorders, for example. Among the well-established findings of this research are that chemical dependency and compulsive gambling are related, that compulsive gamblers will use almost any means to obtain money to gamble, and that the earlier in life a person begins to gamble, the more likely he or she is to develop gambling disorders. For all that has been learned about the causes and consequences of gambling disorders, however, the research on how to treat them is far less conclusive.[40]

More important, progress seems likely in the effort to understand gambling better. The rapid proliferation of legalized gambling is a recent phenomenon. Necessarily, research on most aspects of the subject is at an early stage, and the number of researchers has been relatively small. With a critical mass of scholars from a broad range of disciplines now beginning to concentrate their time and talents on understanding gambling, the historical moment at which a major commitment of research funding and other resources is likely to bear fruit may have arrived.

POLICY RECOMMENDATIONS

Although the federal role in gambling policymaking is much less extensive than the role played by the states, the federal government is uniquely situated to act in certain areas of gambling activity. Consequently, we recommend changes in public policy regarding Internet and sports betting. We also urge the federal government to expand its sponsorship of research about gambling.

INTERNET GAMBLING

The United States should be free of Internet gambling. Although it may be impossible to accomplish this goal in the immediate future, we recommend that the federal government do everything it can to pursue it. We share the view that the president of The Century Foundation, Richard C. Leone, offered in testimony supporting an anti-Internet-gambling bill. In general, Leone said, he is optimistic that "in a decade or two, we shall have a body of well-established law pertaining to many Internet-related issues that now seem esoteric or even baffling." For the time being, however, he regards such legislation as "an important first step to put sand in the wheels, in effect, and make it harder for gambling on line to prosper."[41]

To this end we recommend that Congress make explicit that using Internet-related technologies to gamble is a crime. The Justice Department's argument that the Wire Communications Act of 1961 already covers such activities is strained at best and, in any event, lacks clear statutory status.[42]

In addition, we recommend, as did the National Gambling Impact Study Commission, that Congress pass legislation to render unrecoverable credit card debts incurred through Internet gambling. Banks and other firms that wire money to foreign destinations also should be prevented from transferring depositors' funds to Internet gambling outfits. To be sure, Americans who want desperately to gamble on the Internet will find a way to get their money to the necessary places, perhaps by opening an overseas bank account, then instructing the bank to transfer funds to an Internet gambling firm. But the casual or experimental Internet gambler who has to go to more trouble than entering a credit card number often will be deterred. Aware that the multiplicity of international jurisdictions will complicate the task, we also recommend that every possible diplomatic effort be taken to persuade foreign governments to instruct the Internet operators they license to keep American bettors off of their sites.

SPORTS BETTING

The legal sports betting that goes on in Nevada is merely the tip of the sports betting iceberg: it constitutes no more than 1 to 3 percent of all the sports betting in which Americans take part. In addition, the elimination of the Nevada sports books would not eliminate the widespread distribution of point spreads through the media. Efforts to enact such a ban are largely beside the point—the legislative equivalent of looking for lost keys where the light is rather than where one dropped them.

That said, we strongly recommend that Congress charge the Department of Justice to create a federal task force to propose how federal laws regarding illegal sports betting can be enforced. Among the task force's responsibilities should be to conduct a study of college sports gambling, to advise the NCAA about its role in law enforcement, and to examine the effectiveness of the steps taken by colleges and universities to reduce the problem.

Much also can be accomplished if college and university administrators resolve to take action about a serious problem that they all too often have chosen to ignore. Offices of student affairs should have staff members who investigate student gambling activities and have the authority to recommend expulsion for student bookies and either mandated treatment or, as a last resort, expulsion for chronic illegal gamblers. Students involved in bookmaking operations should be forced to cooperate fully with law enforcement personnel. Campus gambling rings should be treated like campus drug rings. Would college or university administrators wait until drug trafficking led to violence before taking action against it? Of course not; nor should they wait when high-stakes gambling is occurring on campus.

RESEARCH

A great deal of research needs to be done on virtually every aspect of gambling's causes and consequences. State and tribal governments should sponsor some of it, especially concerning the social and economic effects of gambling on cities, states, and tribes. Commercial casinos should continue to sponsor research on gambling disorders and to cooperate fully with any government-sponsored research programs.

But the federal government bears the main responsibility for inaugurating a new round of research, primarily because the rapid rise of legalized gambling is a nationwide phenomenon that has occurred in the absence of reliable information and understanding. To some extent, the new federal role will involve little more than incorporating the study of gambling into ongoing research protocols. Organizations such as the National Institutes of Health, the Substance Abuse and Mental Health Services Administration, and the National Institute of Justice already conduct longitudinal population studies. Congress should instruct them to gather data on the social and economic aspects of gambling. As these data accumulate, they should be made readily available to all interested parties through government websites and academic data archives.

In addition, Congress should strongly urge research-sponsoring agencies such as the National Science Foundation to place a premium on research proposals that will increase scientific understanding of gambling. Commensurately, Congress should give these agencies the budgetary resources to do so. We further recommend that the federal government encourage research on the clinical treatment of gambling disorders, as well as on the work of self-help groups such as Gamblers Anonymous.

Our last recommendation for federal research lies at the intersection of research and Internet gambling. Many aspects of the burgeoning Internet gambling industry need scholarly attention. These include the degree of addiction caused by online gambling and the particular attractiveness of Internet betting to young people, among other topics.

We have described throughout this book the decentralized character of most public policymaking concerning gambling. State and tribal governments, not the government in Washington, have provided the major arenas of politics and policy. But we also have described the effects of the national climate of opinion on gambling's recent spread across the American landscape. It is our hope and our expectation that, as was the case with the 1964 Surgeon General's report on smoking, active federal sponsorship of research on gambling will enhance public understanding of its causes and consequences in ways that will inform and perhaps alter this climate of opinion.

6
CONCLUSION

The spread of legalized gambling across the American landscape was one of the most important transformations to take place in domestic public policy during the latter decades of the twentieth century. In 1960, the United States was a nation with no legal lotteries and, outside of Nevada, no legal casinos. Since then, beginning with New Hampshire in 1964, thirty-eight states and the District of Columbia have created state-sponsored lotteries. In 1976, state-sanctioned commercial casinos began to spread, eventually into eleven states. After a series of judicial and congressional actions during the late 1980s, tribal casinos proliferated on American Indian lands in twenty-four states.

Some common themes have characterized the debates about all of these forms of gambling. Typically, those who support legalization have argued in terms of personal liberty and economic prosperity. Opponents have concentrated much of their fire on issues of social and personal morality, as well as on gambling disorders and their consequences for individuals and society.

In addition to these broad-gauged arguments, each form of gambling has generated its own set of controversies. Lotteries have been championed as a voluntary source of revenue for state governments but criticized for debasing these governments' moral authority by putting them into the gambling business. A "jobs vs. mobs" debate has divided the advocates of commercial casinos, who tout the economic benefits of capital investment and employment, from casino opponents, who point to the crime and other social problems associated with casino gambling. Tribal casinos are portrayed by supporters as a

blessing to economically distressed Native Americans, and by opponents as a curse both to traditional tribal cultures and to surrounding
communities.

In recent years, the pace of gambling legalization has slowed.
Only two states have created lotteries since 1994. Commercial and
tribal casinos spread rapidly during the early 1990s, but less so after-
ward. Meanwhile, at the federal level, the policy agenda has included several efforts to rein in gambling, whether through the creation of
the National Gambling Impact Study Commission or the consideration of laws against Internet gambling and sports betting.

In this brief conclusion, we assess the politics, policy, and
prospects of legalized gambling in the United States. Drawing on the
analysis contained in previous chapters, we take stock of where the
nation has been and where it may be headed in this important area of
public policy. We also summarize our recommendations concerning
where the nation ought to be.

POLITICS

The transformation in public policy toward legalized gambling that
occurred during the latter decades of the twentieth century was in
many ways a classic case of decentralized policymaking within a federal system. Every state lottery and commercial casino owes its existence to a decision made by a state government. Yet the multistate and
multiregional character of this transformation is too apparent to be
coincidental. National political influences clearly have been at work
as well. Indeed, in certain areas—notably tribal, Internet, and sports
gambling—national political influences have been the major force
shaping the politics of gambling. Ascertaining how decentralized policymaking and national political influences have operated in recent
decades may offer clues about whether the recent slowdown in gambling legalization marks a halt or merely a hiatus.

DECENTRALIZED POLICYMAKING

The politics of state policymaking are shaped in many ways by
the internal characteristics of each state. But states do not exist in
isolation from each other. Through the workings of policy diffusion,
state governments share and borrow new approaches to public policy.

Sometimes they do so out of admiration (we call this ordinary diffusion), and sometimes as a strategy to fend off the unwanted consequences of another state's policies (reactive diffusion).

Policy diffusion, mostly of the ordinary kind, has strongly influenced the politics of lotteries: an animated map of state lotteries in the United States from 1964 to 1994 would resemble a spreading ink blot. The diffusion of commercial casinos was more contained, with most casino legalizations occurring in Mississippi River states or their neighbors. In some cases the diffusion of casinos was reactive. Illinois, for example, legalized commercial casinos to keep its citizens' gambling dollars from straying into nearby Iowa.

Of the internal state characteristics that have affected the politics of gambling, economic factors have been prominent. The states' quest for revenues other than sales and income taxes spurred many lottery enactments. Their desire for jobs and capital investment sometimes made commercial casinos appealing as well. Public opinion in each state, in addition to the opinions and efforts of state political leaders, also have been important. In most states, both the people and their leaders have been more likely to support lotteries than casinos, which helps to explain why three-fourths of the states have lotteries while only one-fifth have commercial casinos. In the case of lotteries, a third state characteristic affecting the politics of gambling is size: smaller states suffer unfavorable economies of scale in lottery operations. In the case of casinos, the difficulties of amending state constitutions to remove legal barriers to casino gambling have been especially formidable in many states.

NATIONAL POLITICAL INFLUENCES

National political influences on the politics of gambling have been more apparent in some areas of gambling policy than in others. Because Internet gambling, sports betting, gambling-related research, and tribal gambling fit mostly within the jurisdiction of the federal government, federal laws such as the Indian Gaming Regulatory Act of 1988 and the Professional and Amateur Sports Protection Act of 1992, as well as Supreme Court decisions such as *California v. Cabazon Band of Mission Indians*[1] and *Greater New Orleans Broadcasting Association v. United States*[2] have been visible as well as important. So have the activities of national interest groups such as the American Gaming Association and the National Coalition Against

Legalized Gambling (NCALG). The national climate of opinion—both public opinion and expert opinion—has been the subject of considerable attention in the national news media.

In recent years, much effort and, at least on the part of the casino industry, much money for lobbyists' fees and campaign contributions have been expended in Washington to shape federal policy on a host of gambling issues. These include cracking down on Internet gambling, making sports betting illegal throughout the country, sponsoring and conducting extensive new research on gambling, and expanding (or contracting) the scope of tribal gambling. Unusual political alliances have been formed, such as the one between commercial casino companies and Christian conservative groups, which for different reasons both oppose Internet gambling. Thus far, however, little has been accomplished in the way of new federal legislation.

In less apparent ways, national political influences also have shaped the politics of gambling at the state and tribal levels. The states adopted their lotteries one by one, but the growth in public support for lottery legalization was a national trend. National gambling corporations and, since its formation in 1994, NCALG have lobbied individual state governments that were considering sponsoring lotteries and sanctioning commercial casinos. Similarly, national organizations such as the National Governors' Association (anti) and the National Congress of American Indians (pro) have worked hard to shape the policies of the states toward tribal casinos. The national climate of expert opinion about legalized gambling has been regarded by both supporters and opponents as so important that the creation, statutory authority, and membership of the National Gambling Impact Study Commission were the subjects of pitched political battles in Washington.

POLICY

Whether the spread of legalized gambling has ended or is only experiencing a pause, a tremendous amount of gambling is going on in the United States. We hope the day will come when some forms of gambling either will be repealed—especially lotteries—or suppressed, as we suggest for Internet gambling. In the shorter term, however, we are primarily concerned with what governments can do to improve their existing policies toward gambling. We have offered in this work many policy recommendations. Federal, state, and tribal governments all have much to do.

FEDERAL

Although most public policies concerning gambling are made by the states, the federal government has an important role to play. We believe that Washington should concentrate its efforts on those forms of gambling that it is uniquely situated to address, such as Internet gambling and sports betting. The federal government also should foster research on gambling that will be of value to all levels of government.

In this spirit, we recommend that Congress make research on gambling a priority for several federal agencies. For example, the National Institutes of Health, the National Institute of Justice, and other appropriate federal agencies should be encouraged to gather data about gambling as part of their ongoing longitudinal survey research programs. The National Science Foundation should place a premium on funding research proposals that will increase the scientific understanding of gambling.

With regard to specific forms of gambling, we urge that Congress make explicitly illegal the use of Internet-related technologies to gamble. In addition, Congress should declare as unrecoverable all credit card debts incurred through Internet gambling, and it should spur diplomatic efforts to discourage foreign governments from allowing their Internet gambling operators to accept bets from American citizens.

Concerning sports betting, Congress should charge the Department of Justice to create a federal task force to propose how federal laws regarding illegal sports betting can be enforced. Among the issues the task force should address are problems related to college sports betting.

Finally, Congress should require American Indian tribes to submit relevant information to federal agencies about the effects of their gambling activities on local environments, as well as on tribal economic development and the other purposes listed in the Indian Gaming Regulatory Act.

STATE

The states should never have gotten into the lottery business. The way state governments dilute their moral authority by enticing people to gamble is deplorable, especially considering that the poor, minorities, and the less educated buy lottery tickets at a disproportionately high rate. We strongly urge the twelve states without lotteries to remain as they are, and we await the day when the thirty-eight lottery states will cease to sponsor this form of gambling.

Pending repeal, states with lotteries should conduct them less irresponsibly than they do now. We recommend that states operate lotteries in the same general way that many states already operate liquor stores: offer the service to their citizens without encouraging them to use it. Moreover, states should provide more help to those who have developed gambling disorders or who buy more lottery tickets than they can afford. A good start would be to allocate a substantial portion of lottery revenues to the treatment of gambling disorders.

In order to make their lottery advertising more responsible, states should prominently display accurate information about the probability of winning each game. Likewise, states should not target their advertising to groups that are especially vulnerable to gambling disorders or serious economic loss, especially the poor, minorities, and the less educated.

With regard to state sanctioning of casino gambling, we recommend that state governments proceed cautiously. States without commercial casinos may want to consider casino legalization as a strategy of economic development for depressed areas. No such decision should be made, however, without sound cost-benefit analyses and an extensive public debate that culminates in a statewide referendum.

In states where casinos are legal, we recommend a regulatory approach that more closely resembles the Nevada model, in which casino companies are treated as corporate citizens that require special regulatory attention, than the more stringent New Jersey model. At the very least, because of the corruption that can ensue when state officials control a scarce and highly valuable resource, states should not limit the number of casino licenses in the eligible cities and counties. We further endorse the policy already in effect in some casino states that forces casino companies to match their investments in gambling facilities dollar for dollar with investments in hotel, restaurant, and resort development. Such an approach ensures more capital investment as well as greater employment and managerial opportunities that workers can transfer beyond the casino industry. It also discourages casino companies from entering markets that have no realistic hope of attracting tourists from outside the region.

Finally, states that already permit Class III gambling should fulfill the charge in the Indian Gaming Regulatory Act to negotiate compacts with any remaining tribes that are located within their borders and want to offer gambling on tribal lands. In return, as states negotiate new compacts or renegotiate existing compacts, they should seek funds from tribes to treat gambling disorders, build roads and bridges to accommodate casino-related traffic, and relieve other costs to the state.

TRIBAL

Because we hope that the entry of American Indian tribes into the gambling business will foster the economic independence so long denied to Native Americans, our recommendations to tribal governments are few. In addition to providing requested data to the federal government and sharing some of their profits with state governments, tribes should recognize their responsibility to monitor and ease the negative effects of their gambling operations. For example, we recommend that tribes channel some of their profits from casino gambling into treatment programs for tribal members suffering from gambling disorders.

Most important, tribes should use the proceeds and experience derived from gambling as resources to help diversify their economic base. Specifically, they should diversify their financial investments and use gambling profits as seed money for a wider range of economic enterprises.

PROSPECTS

Has the national trend toward legalized gambling crested, or is it merely in abeyance, perhaps gathering force for another round of expansion? Opponents of gambling can take comfort from the effective work of NCALG, the concerns about gambling disorders expressed in the NGISC's widely publicized report, the recent hesitation of state governments to legalize new forms of gambling, Congress's inclination to focus on proposals for antigambling rather than pro-gambling legislation, and the widespread national prosperity that has reduced the incentives for governments to turn to gambling as a new source of revenue. But gambling's proponents have no reason for permanent despair. More and more Americans regard gambling in casinos and on lotteries as ordinary recreational activities and wonder why they cannot gamble wherever they live or travel. Commercial and tribal gambling interests are steadily increasing their political efforts, both as lobbyists and as campaign contributors. Should another prolonged economic recession occur, gambling revenues may once again become appealing to governments at all levels as an alternative to increased taxes.

As the policy recommendations that conclude the chapters of this book indicate, we in some cases rejoice and in no case mourn the recent loss of momentum on behalf of legalized gambling. Our recommendations also take note that what legalized gambling has experienced is a slowdown, perhaps a halt, but not a reversal. No state has abolished its lottery or expelled its casinos, nor is any state seriously considering doing so. The same is true of tribal governments and the federal government with regard to casinos on American Indian lands. Thus, for prudential reasons, we regard efforts to meliorate existing forms of legal gambling as being no less worthy of serious attention than other, more dramatic proposals.

NOTES

CHAPTER 1

1. Illegal gambling, mostly on sports or through the Internet, is discussed in Chapter 5.

2. *California* v. *Cabazon Band of Mission Indians,* 480 U.S. 202 (1987); *Seminole Tribe of Florida* v. *Florida* 517 U.S. 44 (1996).

CHAPTER 2

1. Charles T. Clotfelter et al., "State Lotteries at the Turn of the Century," report to the National Gambling Impact Study Commission, April 23, 1999, p. 13. This source is available online at http://www.ngisc.gov.

2. See, for example, the results of two decades of polling reported in the *Gallup Poll Monthly* (July 1996), pp. 13–18.

3. In 1996, Arkansas voters defeated a lottery-casino referendum.

4. Richard McGowan, *State Lotteries and Legalized Gambling* (Westport, Conn.: Quorum Books, 1994), Chapter 1.

5. John Samuel Ezell, *Fortune's Merry Wheel: The Lottery in America* (Cambridge, Mass.: Harvard University Press, 1960), p. 16.

6. Charles T. Clotfelter and Philip J. Cook, *Selling Hope: State Lotteries in America* (Cambridge, Mass.: Harvard University Press, 1989), p. 35.

7. Ibid., p. 164.

8. Clotfelter et al., "State Lotteries at the Turn of the Century," p. 6.

9. Clotfelter and Cook, *Selling Hope,* pp. 130–33.

10. Four states—Oregon, Nevada, Delaware, and Montana—had already taken steps to legalize gambling on sports or sports-based lottery games and were exempted from the legislation.

11. Connecticut is the exception: it enacted a personal income tax in 1991.

12. "Gallup Releases Social Audit on Gambling in America," 1999, available at http://www.gallup.com/poll/socialaudits/Gamblingrelease.asp; Abbey Begun, *Gambling: Crime or Recreation* (Detroit: Gale Group, 2000), p. 139. Gallup's question is "As you may know, some states legalize betting so that the state can raise revenues. Please tell me whether you would approve or disapprove of each of the following types of betting as a way to help your state raise revenue. First, would you approve or disapprove of . . . Next, how about . . .?"

13. Commission on the Review of the National Policy toward Gambling, *Gambling in America* (Washington, D.C.: Government Printing Office, 1976).

14. The classic work on diffusion theory is Everett M. Rogers, *Diffusion of Innovation* (New York: W. W. Norton, 1962). The classic application of diffusion theory to state policy innovation is Jack L. Walker, "The Diffusion of Innovations among the American States," *American Political Science Review* 63, no. 3 (1969): 880–99.

15. Clotfelter and Cook, *Selling Hope*, p. 150.

16. Frances Stokes Berry and William D. Berry, "State Lottery Adoptions as Policy Innovations: An Event History Analysis," *American Political Science Review* 84, no. 2 (1990): 395–412.

17. Clotfelter and Cook, *Selling Hope*, Chapter 9; Nicholas Thompson, "Snake Eyes: Even Education Programs Can't Redeem State Lotteries," *Washington Monthly*, December 1999, pp. 14–19.

18. Frances Stokes Berry, "Sizing Up State Policy Innovation Research," *Policy Studies Journal* 22, no. 4 (1994): 442–56.

19. Virginia Gray, "Innovation in the States: A Diffusion Study," *American Political Science Review* 67, no. 4 (1973): 1174–85.

20. John Lyman Mason and Michael Nelson, *The Politics of Gambling: State Policy Innovation in the American South* (Baltimore: Johns Hopkins University Press, forthcoming). See also Michael Mintrom, *Policy Entrepreneurs and School Choice* (Washington, D.C.: Georgetown University Press, 2000).

21. Berry and Berry, "State Lottery Adoptions," 395–412. The Berrys measured fiscal health as the ratio of total state revenue minus total state spending to total state spending. Clotfelter and Cook (*Selling Hope*, p. 149) found that the fiscal health of a state was uncorrelated with its adopting or not adopting a lottery. But their measure of fiscal health involved only revenues, not spending. An additional finding of the Berrys is that the greater the average personal income in a state, the more likely that a lottery will be enacted. They explain this finding by claiming that politicians do not think a lottery can be successful in a state where income is below a certain level.

22. This description is consistent with a finding reported in Berry and Berry, "State Lottery Adoptions as Policy Innovations."

23. Thompson, "Snake Eyes," p. 17.

24. Clotfelter et al., "State Lotteries at the Turn of the Century," p. 4.

25. Stanley M. Cherwin, "The Lure of the Lottery—Tennessee's Last Hope?" *State Tax Notes*, October 4, 1999.

26. Clotfelter et al., "State Lotteries at the Turn of the Century," p. 12.

27. National Gambling Impact Study Commission (NGISC), *Final Report* (Washington, D.C.: U.S. Government Printing Office,1999), 3:17.

28. Cherwin, "The Lure of the Lottery."

29. Clotfelter and Cook, *Selling Hope*, Chapter 12. See also Clotfelter et al., "State Lotteries at the Turn of the Century," pp. 22–23.

30. NGISC, *Final Report*, 2:3.

31. Clotfelter et al., "State Lotteries at the Turn of the Century," p. 18.

32. Cherwin, "The Lure of the Lottery."

33. NGISC, *Final Report*, 3:23.

34. Cherwin, "The Lure of the Lottery."

35. Clotfelter and Cook, *Selling Hope*, p. 113.

36. Ibid., p. 228.

37. Clotfelter et al., "State Lotteries at the Turn of the Century," p. 12.

38. NGISC, *Final Report*, 3:5.

39. Thompson, "Snake Eyes."

40. In September 2000, the former computer manager of the Kansas lottery was indicted for stealing more than $62,000 by converting losing instant scratch-off tickets into winners.

41. Samuel Huntington, *American Politics: The Promise of Disharmony* (Cambridge, Mass.: Harvard University Press, 1981).

42. We believe that the Supreme Court's traditionally broad interpretation of the interstate commerce clause would allow the federal government to assume a role in areas such as multistate lotteries and lottery advertising.

43. Complete adherence to the state-run liquor store model would suggest that advertising by lottery agencies should be banned. But the products state-run liquor stores sell are widely advertised by their manufacturers. Rather than recommend, in pursuance of this model, that the corporations that create lottery games bear the responsibility to advertise, we prefer that advertising remain in the hands of state lottery agencies.

CHAPTER 3

1. The data in this paragraph come from Abbey Begun, *Gambling: Crime or Recreation?* (Detroit: Gale Group, 2000), Chapter 4.

2. Off-track betting, whether at betting shops or, in some states, by telephone, occurs at sites where there is no racing. Simulcast wagering typically involves bets placed at one track on races run at another. A hybrid of the two, now legal in nine states, is account wagering, in which bettors who

sign up for "closed-door subscriber-based" systems can open accounts at racing venues and bet by telephone or, in some states, through the Internet.

3. The 1997 amount is adjusted for inflation.

4. Tennessee legalized horse racing in 1987, then repealed the law twelve years later when no potential track owner found the prospect of a new track to be a profitable investment.

5. Electronic gaming devices (EGDs) emerged in the early 1980s from the same technology that produced Pac-Man and other video games. EGDs come in many forms, including video poker, video keno, and slot machines, and are found in a variety of legal and illegal settings, such as truck stops, bars, restaurants, and lodge halls. Until outlawed by the state supreme court in South Carolina in 1999, video poker parlors operated virtually as casinos in that state. As noted in Chapter 2, some states have incorporated video gambling into their lotteries.

6. Ronald M. Pavalko, *Risky Business: America's Fascination with Gambling* (Belmont, Calif.: Wadsworth/Thompson Learning, 1999), p. 101.

7. Card rooms, in which bettors rent a seat to play games such as poker and blackjack with other bettors, are another form of legal gambling that until recently had been flourishing. Because the great majority of card room gambling takes place in California, however, it seems fated to experience a severe decline in the aftermath of the state's decision in 2000 to legalize tribal casinos.

8. National Gambling Impact Study Commission (NGISC), *Final Report* (Washington, D.C.: Government Printing Office, 1999), 3:5. The Nevada model came into being in the late 1950s, when the state replaced its counties as casino regulators.

9. John Dombrink and William N. Thompson, *The Last Resort: Success and Failure in Campaigns for Casinos* (Reno and Las Vegas: University of Nevada Press, 1990), p. 28.

10. NGISC, *Final Report*, 3:5–6.

11. A referendum is a ballot measure placed before the voters by the state legislature. An initiative gets on the ballot by citizen petition, bypassing the legislature.

12. The director of the Public Gaming Research Institute, for example, predicted in 1977 that casinos would be legal in six states by 1980. In 1980, an institute report predicted that nine states would have legal casinos by 1984, and eighteen states would by 1989. A Paine Webber vice president predicted that during the 1980s, "10 to 20 states will legalize gaming." Dombrink and Thompson, *The Last Resort*, pp. 90–92.

13. Ibid., Chapters 3–7.

14. 480 U.S. 202 (1987).

15. As discussed in Chapter 4, tribal casinos operating on sovereign tribal lands cannot be taxed or regulated by state governments.

16. Colorado is one exception: in 1990, following South Dakota's example, it legalized small-stakes casino gambling, in part to help restore historic towns. Casinos are legal in Cripple Creek, Black Hawk, and Central City. The other two exceptions, Indiana and Michigan, are discussed later in the chapter.

17. Robert Goodman, *The Luck Business: The Devastating Consequences and Broken Promises of America's Gambling Explosion* (New York: Free Press, 1995), p. 97.

18. NGISC, *Final Report*, 2:7.

19. David S. Broder, *Democracy Derailed: Initiative Campaigns and the Power of Money* (New York: Harcourt, 2000), pp. 78–81.

20. John Branston, "Against All Odds," *Memphis*, September 1997, p. 34.

21. In 1996, Louisiana enacted a constitutional amendment that gave voters the right to hold local referenda on casino and video poker gambling. Later that year, thirty-four of sixty-four parishes voted to expel video poker, and fourteen voted not to allow riverboat casinos. None of the six parishes that already had riverboat casinos voted to expel them, nor did New Orleans vote against its land-based casino.

22. Timothy L. O'Brien, *Bad Bet: The Inside Story of the Glamour, Glitz, and Danger of America's Gambling Industry* (New York: Random House, 1998), p. 120.

23. Essentially, these acts require casinos to report to the federal government any amounts above $10,000 that they pay or receive.

24. NGISC, *Final Report*, 3:12–15.

25. 527 U.S. 173 (1999).

26. Concerned at the decline of the horse racing industry, Congress also passed the Interstate Horseracing Act of 1978, which allowed racetracks to cooperate across state lines in offering simulcast betting.

27. Allen J. Cigler and Burdett A. Loomis, "Organized Interests and the Search for Certainty," in Allen J. Cigler and Burdett A. Loomis, eds., *Interest Group Politics,* 3d ed. (Washington, D.C.: CQ Press, 1991), pp. 385–98.

28. The act granted the commission power to subpoena documents but not persons, even though Charles H. Morin, the chair of the NGISC's 1976 predecessor, the Commission on the Review of the National Policy toward Gambling, told Congress, "Such a Commission is meaningless without this power." Melissa Weinstein Kaye, "Smooth Sailing Is Expected for Gambling Commission," *CQ Weekly Report*, July 20, 1996, pp. 2053–55.

29. Donald L. Barlett and James B. Steele, "Throwing the Games," *Time,* September 25, 2000.

30. Tellingly, NCALG , unlike the AGA, does not rate an entry in Immanuel Ness, *Encyclopedia of Interest Groups and Lobbyists in the United States* (Cambridge, Mass.: M. E. Sharpe, 2000).

31. These data from the Gallup poll are reported in *Gambling—Crime or Recreation?* (Wylie, Tex.: Information Plus, 1998), p. 141. The question was: "As you may know, some states legalize betting so that the state can raise revenues. Please tell me whether you would approve or disapprove of the following types of betting as a way to help your state raise revenue."

32. Some casino critics have used a different term for this process: a race to the bottom.

33. Dombrink and Thompson, *The Last Resort*, pp. 183–84.

34. Ibid., Chapter 4.

35. Professors Patrick A. Pierce and Donald E. Miller of St. Mary's College have found that the presence of a lottery in a state increases the probability that the state will legalize commercial casinos. "Roll the Dice: Internal Diffusion of Gambling Policy in the American States" (unpublished manuscript).

36. William N. Thompson and Ricardo Gazel, "*The Last Resort* Revisited: The Spread of Gambling as a Dilemma," in William Eadington and Judy Cornelius, eds., *Gambling: Public Policy and the Social Sciences* (Reno: University of Nevada Press, 1997), pp. 183–206.

37. Dombrink and Thompson, *The Last Resort*, pp. 130–31.

38. In some states, constitutional barriers to casinos had been removed during the 1970s and 1980s as a by-product of constitutional amendments to permit state lotteries.

39. Protecting his domain, Atlantic City casino owner Donald Trump financed much of the opposition lobbying in New York.

40. The Arkansas ballot measure also would have created a state lottery and legalized gambling in four counties that do not have a racetrack.

41. Gallup poll, "Gambling in America," available at http://www.gallup.com/poll/socialaudits/Gamblingrelease.asp.

42. General Accounting Office, *Campaign Finance: Contributions from Gambling Interests Have Increased* (Washington, D.C.: U.S. Government Printing Office, 1999).

43. O'Brien, *Bad Bet*, p. 220.

44. National Opinion Research Council, "Gambling Impact and Behavior Study," report to the National Gambling Impact Study Commission, April 1, 1999, pp. 70, 76–77, available at http://www.ngisc.gov. The appeal of this study to casino advocates is that it was commissioned by a government entity. As discussed later in this chapter and in Chapter 5, the study's findings are not uncontroversial.

45. NGISC, *Final Report*, 4:1.

46. Ibid., 4:4.

47. Ibid., 7:6, 27–28.

48. W. Dale Mason, *Indian Gaming: Tribal Sovereignty and American Politics* (Norman: University of Oklahoma Press, 2000).

49. Ibid., 3:5–6.
50. Ibid., 3:18.

CHAPTER 4

1. National Gambling Impact Study Commission (NGISC), *Final Report,* (Washington, D.C.: Government Printing Office), Chapter 2.
2. Ibid., 6:2.
3. 30 U.S. (5 Pet.) 1 (1831).
4. 30 U.S. 515 (1832).
5. *United States* v. *Sioux Nation of Indians,* 448 U.S. 371, 415 (1980).
6. NGISC, *Final Report,* 6:5-6
7. In the 1960s, as part of President Lyndon B. Johnson's war on poverty, a few tribes applied for and successfully administered community development grants designed to attract industry to reservations. See Fergus Bordewich, *Killing the White Man's Indian: Reinventing Native Americans at the End of the Twentieth Century* (New York: Doubleday, 1996), pp. 302–33.
8. For example, the Dawes Severalty Act (1887) forced tribes to convert lands held in common into individually owned farms and rigorously encouraged English literacy and Christianity among Native Americans. Many tribes resisted these attempts at assimilation.
9. The ruling, by the Fifth Circuit Court of Appeals, was in the case of *Seminole Tribe of Florida* v. *Butterworth,* 658 F.2d 310 (1981).
10. 447 U.S. 134, 154 (1980).
11. Timothy L. O'Brien, *Bad Bet: The Inside Story of the Glamour, Glitz, and Danger of America's Gambling Industry* (New York: Random House), p. 139.
12. Stephen Cornell, et al., *American Indian Gaming Policy and Its Socio-Economic Effects* (Cambridge, Mass.: Economic Resource Group, 1998), pp. 11–12. The majority of federally recognized tribes—more than 300—are in Alaska. None of them have Class III gambling operations. The National Gambling Impact Study Commission found that in 1997 the twenty largest Indian gambling facilities—around one-thirteenth of all such facilities—accounted for 50.5 percent of total tribal gambling revenues. The 105 largest Indian gambling facilities—around two-fifths of all such facilities—accounted for 91.7 percent of total revenues. NGISC, *Final Report,* 6:3.
13. Because some of the tribes that own casinos are very small and some of the tribes that do not are quite large, the 84 percent of lower-forty-eight tribes that own casinos include only 34 percent of all American Indians living on reservations. Cornell et al., *American Indian Gaming Policy,* p. 12.
14. The data are for 1996. General Accounting Office, *Casino Gaming Regulation: Roles of Five States and the National Indian Gaming Commission* (Washington, D.C.: Government Printing Office), 1998, p. 4.

15. See Jeff Benedict, *Without Reservation: The Making of America's Most Powerful Indian Tribe and Foxwoods, the World's Largest Casino* (New York: HarperCollins, 2000); Kim Isaac Eisler, *Revenge of the Pequots: How a Small Native American Tribe Created the World's Most Profitable Casino* (New York: Simon and Schuster, 2001).

16. The Pequots agreed to allow the Mohegon tribe to open a casino in Montville, Connecticut, in exchange for the state's agreement to lower the Foxwoods casino's minimum annual payment to the state treasury to $80 million.

17. W. Dale Mason, *Indian Gaming: Tribal Sovereignty and American Politics* (Norman, Okla.: University of Oklahoma Press, 2000).

18. *Seminole Tribe of Florida v. Florida*, 517 U.S. 44 (1996). In this case, the Court divided along conservative-liberal lines, with conservative justices in the majority.

19. In contrast, neighboring Arizona's disunited tribes have been unable to secure any casino agreements with the state government. Mason, *Indian Gaming*, Chapters 3–5.

20. David Plotz, "Jackpot," *New Republic*, March 13, 2000, pp. 26-29; and Todd S. Purdum, "Indian Tribes Approve Gambling Compacts with California," *New York Times*, September 11, 1999.

21. *Seminole Tribe of Florida v. Butterworth*.

22. Robert Goodman, *The Luck Business: The Devastating Consequences and Broken Promises of America's Gambling Explosion* (New York: Free Press, 1995), pp. 108, 110. Goodman expresses some concerns about tribal gambling, however, including the possibility that states will legalize commercial casinos in order to drive tribal casinos out of business.

23. Cornell et al., *American Indian Gaming Policy*, p. 8.

24. Quoted in David S. Broder, *Democracy Derailed: Initiative Campaigns and the Power of Money* (New York: Harcourt, 2000), pp. 81–82.

25. John Kruger, "FEC Ruling Could Trigger Flood of Money from Indian Tribes," *The Hill*, June 27, 2000.

26. Elizabeth Arnold, "Native Americans and Politics," *Morning Edition*, National Public Radio, July 12, 2000.

27. Because their lands are in sparsely populated Plains and Rocky Mountain states, most tribes would not profit from casinos if they had them.

28. Brett Pulley, "Tribes Weigh Tradition Against Growth of Casino Resorts," *New York Times*, March 16, 1999.

29. Goodman, *The Luck Business*, p. 120.

30. NGISC, *Final Report*, 6:11.

31. David Johnston, "Prosecutor Clears Babbitt in Casino Inquiry," *New York Times*, October 14, 1999.

32. General Accounting Office, *Casino Gaming Regulation*, p. 5. Some of these are in California and will soon be covered by the state's new, initiative-approved policy toward compacts.

33. Mason found that the Department of Justice entrusted great discretion in these matters to local U.S. attorneys. Mason, *Tribal Gaming*, pp. 238–42.
34. Goodman, *The Luck Business*, p. 109.
35. Plotz, "Jackpot," pp. 26–29.
36. NGISC, *Final Report*, pp. 4–11.
37. Ibid., p. 7:9.
38. We thank Dee Garceau, an historian at Rhodes College, for drawing our attention to the tribes' perspective on this question.
39. NGISC, *Final Report*, p. 6:21.

CHAPTER 5

1. Kim Isaac Eisler, *Revenge of the Pequots: How a Small Native American Tribe Created the World's Most Profitable Casino* (New York: Simon and Schuster, 2001)
2. National Gambling Impact Study Commission (NGISC), *Final Report* (Washington, D.C.: U.S. Government Printing Office), 1:6.
3. Jason N. Ader and Marc Falcone, *Gaming Industry* (New York: Bear Stearns Co., 2000), pp. 7–8.
4. Evan I. Schwartz, "Wanna Bet?" *Wired*, October 1995.
5. NGISC, *Final Report*, 2:15.
6. Abbey Begun, *Gambling: Crime or Recreation?* (Detroit: Gale Group, 2000), p. 135; NGISC, *Final Report*, 5:1.
7. NGISC, *Final Report*, 5:1. See also Mark Landler, "Web Comes Up Fast on the Outside," *New York Times*, March 18, 2001.
8. Richard Raysman and Peter Brown, "Congress May Play Its Hand with Internet Gambling Law," *New York Law Journal*, May 9, 2000, pp. 3ff.
9. NGISC, *Final Report*, 3:3.
10. Ibid., 5:7–9.
11. Ader and Falcone, *Gaming Industry*, p. 5.
12. Begun, *Gambling*, p. 145.
13. Marilyn Geewax, "Bill a Net Gain for Gambling, Foes Charge," *Atlanta Journal-Constitution*, June 16, 2000. In a last-minute attempt to mute these objections, the bill was altered to confine its coverage to "otherwise lawful, state-regulated pari-mutuel wagering." Andrew Beyer, "On Internet Bill, All Bets Are Off," *Washington Post*, July 26, 2000.
14. Raysman and Brown, "Congress May Play Its Hand with Internet Gambling Law."
15. Begun, *Gambling*, p. 35.
16. Timothy L. O'Brien, *Bad Bet: The Inside Story of the Glamour, Glitz, and Danger of America's Gambling Industry* (New York: Random House), pp. 228–29.
17. Begun, *Gambling*, p. 132.

18. "Congress Puts a Limit on Sports-Based Lotteries," *Congressional Quarterly Almanac* (Washington, D.C.: Congressional Quarterly Press, 1992), p. 219.

19. In most sporting contests, one team will be favored from the start. Bookies, who must try to keep the betting balanced equally between the teams, offer points to those who bet for the underdog. For example, when the line is Rams +6, the bettor who bets on the Rams only collects money if the Rams win by at least seven points. If the Rams lose, or win by fewer than six points, the bettor loses his money. If the Rams win by six points no money changes hands.

20. O'Brien, *Bad Bet*, pp. 245–46.

21. Begun, *Gambling*, p. 138.

22. Ben Gose, "A Dangerous Bet on Campus," *Chronicle of Higher Education*, April 7, 2000, pp. A49–A51.

23. Ibid., p. A51.

24. Robert Macy, "More Young People Being Introduced to Gambling on College Campuses," *Associated Press Wire Service*, November 10, 1998.

25. "Congress Puts a Limit on Sports-Based Lotteries," p. 219.

26. Begun, *Gambling*, p. 133; "Probation for Former Cop in Sports Betting Network," *New York Daily News*, April 6, 1999.

27. NGISC, *Final Report*, 3:10.

28. Begun, *Gambling*, p. 134.

29. As for sports betting by college students, the National Association of Student Personnel Administrators (NASPA) has pledged to organize a committee to look into gambling among college students. Gose, "A Dangerous Bet on Campus," p. A50.

30. *Folding to the Casino Industry: How Soft Money Buys Congress*, report published by Public Citizen's Congress Watch, Washington, D.C., March 15, 2001.

31. Laurence Arnold, "Newspaper Group Doubts Betting Ban Would Stop Point Spreads," *Associated Press Wire Service*, June 9, 2000.

32. NGISC, *Final Report*, Cover Letter.

33. Ibid., 1:6.

34. Ibid., 1:7.

35. Ibid., 7:3.

36. See, for example, John Samuel Ezell, *Fortune's Merry Wheel: The Lottery in America* (Cambridge, Mass.: Harvard University Press, 1960); Ann Fabian, *Card Sharps, Dream Books, and Bucket Shops: Gambling in Nineteenth-Century America* (Ithaca, N.Y.: Cornell University Press, 1990). The Gallup organization has regularly conducted extensive surveys of Americans' attitudes and activities concerning gambling.

37. NGISC, *Final Report*, 7:2.

38. Ronald M. Pavalko, *Risky Business: America's Fascination with Gambling* (Belmont, Calif.: Wadsworth/Thompson Learning, 1999), p. 55. The works of Clotfelter and Cook and Abt, Smith, and Christiansen are notable exceptions. See Charles T. Clotfelter and Philip J. Cook, *Selling Hope: State Lotteries in America* (Cambridge, Mass.: Harvard University Press, 1989); Vicki Abt, James F. Smith, and Eugene Martin Christiansen, *The Business of Risk: Commercial Gambling in Mainstream America* (Lawrence: University of Kansas Press, 1985).

39. "Gambling Under Attack," *CQ Researcher,* September 6, 1996, pp. 769–92.

40. Good accounts of the research on gambling disorders may be found in Pavalko, *Risky Business*, Chapters 9–10; NGISC, *Final Report*, Chapter 4.

41. Testimony of Richard Leone, June 20, 2000, provided to the authors by The Century Foundation.

42. The current convenience of lottery ticket sales makes it unlikely that the Internet would be an important source of lottery ticket sales in the future. Consistent with our hope that the Internet will become gambling-free, however, we endorse the ban on lottery ticket sales over the Internet found in the House version of the Kyl bill.

CHAPTER 6

1. 480 U.S. 202 (1987).
2. 527 U.S. 173 (1999).

INDEX

Account wagering, 107–8*n*2
Advertising: for commercial casinos, 40; laws on, 12, 40; for lotteries, 12, 22–23, 27–28
AGA. *See* American Gaming Association
Air travel, gambling during, 40
Alabama, lotteries in, 6, 17
Amateur Sports Integrity Act (proposed), 89–90
American Gaming Association (AGA): accomplishments of, 41; formation of, 41; on Internet gambling, 84; strategies of, 41
American Indian Movement, 58–59, 66
Ames, William, 8
Arizona: lotteries in, 10*t*, 19*t*; tribal casinos in, 45, 112*n*19
Arkansas: commercial casinos in, 45–46, 110*n*40; lotteries in, 6, 17, 105*n*3
Auerbach, Red, 87

Babbitt, Bruce, 73, 74
Bank Secrecy Act, 40

Beckerman, Michael, 88
Berry, Frances, 15
Berry, William, 15
Bettors, lottery, demographics of, 18, 21*t*, 25
Big Game lottery, 11, 24
Bingo: charitable, 30–31; tribal, 59
Black Sox Scandal, 86
Bradley, Bill, 89
Brown, Peter, 85
Byrne, Brendan, 34

Cabazon Band of Mission Indians, California v., 35, 60
California: lotteries in, 10*t*, 19*t*; Proposition 1A of, 57, 65; Proposition 5 of, 64; Proposition 13 of, 13; tribal gambling in, 45, 57, 60, 64–65, 75
California v. *Cabazon Band of Mission Indians*, 35, 60
Card rooms, 108*n*7
Carlin, John, 15
Casinos. *See* Commercial casino(s); Tribal gambling
Charitable gambling, 30–31

Note: Page references followed by the letters *f*, *n*, and *t* indicate figures, end notes, and tables, respectively.

117